THE
ESSENTIAL
Labrador Retriever

Consulting Editor

IAN DUNBAR, PH.D., MRCVS

Featuring Photographs by

RENÉE STOCKDALE

HOWELL
BOOK
HOUSE

Howell Book House

A Simon & Schuster Macmillan Company
1633 Broadway
New York, NY 10019

Macmillan Publishing books may be purchased for business or sales promotional use. For information please write: Special Markets Department, Macmillan Publishing USA, 1633 Broadway, New York, NY 10019.

Library of Congress Cataloging-in-Publication Data
The essential Labrador retriever/featuring photographs by Renée Stockdale
   p. cm.
ISBN 0-87605-342-8
1. Labrador retriever   I. Howell Book House.
SF429.L3E77   1998   98-3416
636.752'7—dc21   CIP

Manufactured in the United States of America
10 9 8 7 6 5 4 3 2 1

Series Directors: Dominique DeVito, Donald Stevens
Series Assistant Directors: Jennifer Liberts, Amanda Pisani
Editorial Assistant: Michele Matrisciani
Photography Editor: Sarah Storey
Photography:
   Front cover photo by Winter Churchill Photography; back cover photo by Close Encounters of the Furry Kind/J. Harrison.
   Courtesy of Diana Robinson: 75, 78, 79
   All other photos by Renée Stockdale
Production Team: Heather Pope, Linda Quigley, Chris Van Camp

ESSENTIAL LABRADOR RETRIEVER QUICK REFERENCE CARD

Your Dog's Name _____

Name on Your Dog's Pedigree (if applicable) _____

Where Your Dog Was Purchased _____

   Address _____

   Phone Number _____

Your Dog's Birthday _____

Your Dog's Veterinarian _____

   Address _____

   Phone Number _____

   Emergency Number _____

Your Dog's Health

   VACCINES

      Type _____ *Date Given* __/__/___

      Type _____ *Date Given* __/__/___

      Type _____ *Date Given* __/__/___

      Type _____ *Date Given* __/__/___

   HEARTWORM

      Date Tested __/__/___   *Type Used* _____   *Start Date* __/__/___

Your Dog's License Number _____

Groomer's Name and Phone Number _____

Dog Sitter/Walker's Name and Phone Number _____

Muzzle

Stop

Cheek

Skull

Shoulder

Crest

Wrist

Neck

Forearm

Withers

Pastern

Back

Elbow

Stifle or Knee

Loin

Croup

Hock

Toes

Getting to Know Your Labrador Retriever

If Labs could place personal ads in newspapers looking for their owners, the ad might read something like this:

> NYLP (nice yellow lab pup) seeks owner with lots of free time who loves to hike, swim, run and play!

IS A LAB FOR YOU?

If you get a Lab and you don't really have the time to spend with him, you will probably have problems. Labradors need to go to homes where working with and caring for the dog is looked upon as fun, not a chore. Their appetite for attention is almost insatiable.

The Labrador Retriever is not, as he's often called, "the perfect pet." Some people say, "Labs are great: They're low maintenance." This is not entirely true. Labs may be low maintenance from the standpoint of grooming: Their coats will almost take care of themselves. Also, they are generally healthy and hardy with

Labradors aren't content to live a solitary life outside—they want to come in and be a part of the family!

few inherent health problems. They are, however, high maintenance because they require and demand plenty of your time and attention.

A Labrador Retriever will not be ignored. You should have chosen a Lab because you are going to incorporate your dog into your life: You like to be outdoors, go for walks and play fetch, and you want to learn to do obedience work.

GENERAL CHARACTERISTICS

The Labrador Retriever is one of the most lovable, even-tempered breeds ever developed. Described as a

medium-size sporting dog, the Lab is larger and hardier than the Spaniels of the Sporting Group and smaller in height but stockier than the Setters. The Lab is smaller and has fewer inherent health problems than some of the giant breeds.

Friendly

A well-bred Labrador sees everyone as his friend. Labradors originally were used to retrieve personal belongings as well as fish that fell off the hooks and out of the nets of their masters. Over the years, this instinct was fostered, rewarded and encouraged. The early breeders, of course, tried to cement this instinct with careful, selective breeding, so today you will be hard pressed to find a Labrador that doesn't want to retrieve things or just carry around something in his mouth. Well bred is the key. The source of your Labrador can make all the difference in the world.

Intelligent

Labrador Retrievers are very intelligent, which is why they are the most popular breed used today for guiding the blind and for detecting arson, explosives and drugs. They are unflappable, have a willingness to

CHARACTERISTICS OF THE LABRADOR RETRIEVER

- Active
- Intelligent, fast learner
- Always eager to please
- Tendency to chew destructively
- Few inherent health problems
- Minimal grooming requirements
- Demands a high level of attention

please and have a sturdy constitution. Labradors are also active, bouncy and curious. The word *busy* really sums up Lab pups. They have

A Labrador's high level of intelligence and natural retrieving instincts make him a natural sporting dog.

A Dog's Senses

Sight: Dogs can detect movement at a greater distance than we can, but they can't see as well up close. They can also see better in less light, but they can't distinguish many colors.

Sound: Dogs can hear about four times better than we can, and they can hear high-pitched sounds especially well. They have a wide range of vocalizations, including barks, whimpers, moans and whines.

Smell: A dog's nose is his greatest sensory organ. His sense of smell is so great he can follow a trail that's weeks old, detect odors diluted to one-millionth the concentration we'd need to notice them, even sniff out a person under water!

Taste: Dogs have fewer taste buds than we do, so they're likelier to try anything—and usually do, which is why it's especially important for their owners to monitor their food intake. Dogs are omnivores, which means they eat meat as well as vegetable matter like grasses.

Touch: Dogs are social animals and love to be petted, groomed and played with.

lots of energy, and if it's not channeled properly, they'll find something on their own to do that could be destructive. They need plenty of exercise and stimulation.

The Importance of Training

A puppy should not go out the door without the new owner understanding the importance of training right from the start. With this breed, it's important to establish yourself as the dominant figure from day one. If Labs get the idea even for one minute that they are in charge, you're in for years of unpleasant experiences. You'll be cheating yourself and your Labrador of the wonderful relationship you both deserve.

Setting Limits

You must lay down the law right from the start about what is and isn't acceptable behavior. Just as children cannot grow up to be well-adjusted, solid citizens without the help, love and guidance of caring parents, Labradors cannot raise themselves. They're very resourceful animals and will find ways to entertain themselves.

A Lab must be taught, socialized and loved. A puppy kindergarten class, after the pup's last shots, can be a wonderful learning experience for all.

BEST AS BUDDIES

If you're looking for a guard dog, the Labrador isn't the breed for you. They don't have the same protective instinct as a Shepherd or a Rottweiler. It is, however, typical of a Lab to bark if someone is outside where he cannot see or if he hears a strange noise. This friendly temperament is the most wonderful aspect of the breed and is one of the reasons they are so popular as family dogs.

Again, good breeding is the key. Even though your Lab may accidentally knock over your child with his strong, jubilant tail, you won't have to worry about him attacking or biting in a protective manner. It's not part of a Lab's makeup.

Labradors are active, smart and fast learners. They can be stubborn but can be easily persuaded to see things your way with encouragement and praise. Labradors want to please. They will work eagerly for food rewards but just as eagerly or more for your praise. They love to have something to carry around, and

Labs have lots of energy, so training is necessary to direct that exuberance in the right direction.

playing fetch is usually a favorite game. Labs also have a very keen sense of smell. Their eyesight and hearing are also highly developed, but their noses seem to be their guiding force.

The Labrador's friendly and trusting nature makes him a better buddy than guard dog.

5

CHAPTER TWO

Homecoming

What your new Labrador puppy will need most from you is your time and understanding. Plan to bring your puppy home when you have ample time to spend on acclimating her to her new surroundings. Remember, until the day you bring her home, she will have had the security of her mother and littermates.

When you take your puppy for a checkup, and you should do so as soon as possible after getting her,

your veterinarian will probably have an opinion on what and how to feed your puppy. Pick a veterinarian you can work with and trust. Follow your breeder's advice as much as possible. Select a training method, or enroll in a puppy kindergarten (after the pup's last shots). Most of all, be consistent. Don't change foods every few weeks. Don't overwhelm the puppy with too long a training session at too early an age, and don't try six different training methods in two weeks. Be sensible and don't get carried away with your enthusiasm.

WHERE TO GET YOUR PUPPY

If you buy your puppy from a breeder, chances are the breeder will give you a diet and feeding instructions. And, the pup probably will have had her initial shots and a worming.

You should seek out a puppy from a private breeder who is breeding for the total Labrador. Look for breeders who show their dogs and do some obedience work as well as hunting retriever tests. When looking for a family pet, steer away from dogs bred strictly for fieldwork or field trials. The field trial dogs of today are high-energy dogs and are difficult in a home environment.

It's important to see the mother, or *bitch*, of a litter. If your puppy is raised by a pleasant mother dog who has been allowed to play with, discipline and teach her puppy manners, chances are you'll wind up with a nice dog.

Check out your puppy thoroughly, making sure she's active,

Start training your puppy at an early age, but keep the sessions short to match her limited attention span.

7

friendly and healthy looking, that is, no runny nose or eyes.

Hunting Dogs

When looking for a companion and family pet that may also be used for hunting, people make the common mistake of searching for a field trial breeder. This type may not yield the best match. Instead, look for a breeder who is breeding for a well-rounded Labrador; a well-built, sturdy dog with a willing, pleasant attitude; a dog that will be happy to go out for a day of hunting or retrieving and then equally happy to go home and sleep in front of your fireplace.

PUPPIES FOR SALE

When you buy your puppy from a breeder, check out the surroundings to make sure they seem clean and healthy and ask to see the puppy's mother.

8

PUPPY-PROOFING

It's very important that you puppy-proof your house. When you're home and your puppy's housetraining has gotten underway, she must be able to follow you around and learn right from wrong. Tape up electrical cords out of the way. Find out if any plants in your house are poisonous; if so, put them high up or do without them for a while. A few common houseplants that are poisonous are English ivy, foxglove, hydrangeas, the rootstalk of the iris plant, lily of the valley, philoden-

dron, diffenbachia and many ferns. Remove poisonous plants in your yard or a surrounding area that pose a threat to your puppy.

Keep all household cleaning products safely locked up or out of reach. Also, medications, whether canine or human, should be well labeled and kept out of harm's way. A crate is an essential "safe-haven" for your puppy. If you go out and forget to put the floor wax away, you won't come home to find that your pup has eaten a quart of it and the plastic bottle it came in if she has been safely confined.

Because they are friendly and curious, Labs are easily lured away by a passing jogger, by children on their way to school, by ducks on their way to water and by a host of other things. Labradors in suburbia need a fenced-in yard or a dog run where they will be safe when you're not around. Your Labrador should never be staked or chained on a line with a runner.

TOYS

Give your puppy toys of her own. When your puppy is in her crate, you may opt for very hard rubber balls or Kong toys because they are virtually indestructible. Sterilized natural bones are also good toys.

BISCUITS

Feel free to give your Lab hard dog biscuits as a treat. You can occasionally give your dog a big joint or knuckle bone from the butcher, but only after it has been blanched.

HOUSETRAINING

Labradors are naturally smart and clean. They usually housetrain easily if you are consistent with them. Don't give your puppy the run of the house. Pick a room, like a kitchen or playroom with an easy-to-clean floor and a door to the outside area where you want your puppy to get used to relieving herself. Each time you take the puppy out the door, say "outside, good puppy." Let her relieve herself, and then praise her profusely with "good puppy, good puppy!" in a high-pitched, happy voice.

SUPPLIES

You will need the following equipment: a collar, an identification tag,

HOUSEHOLD DANGERS

Curious puppies and inquisitive dogs get into trouble not because they are bad, but simply because they want to investigate the world around them. It's our job to protect our dogs from harmful substances, like the following:

In the House

cleaners, especially pine oil

perfumes, colognes, aftershaves

medications, vitamins

office and craft supplies

electric cords

chicken or turkey bones

chocolate

some house and garden plants, like ivy, oleander and poinsettia

In the Garage

antifreeze

garden supplies, like snail and slug bait, pesticides, fertilizers, mouse and rat poisons

a leash, water and food bowls, a crate, some toys and perhaps an exercise pen. All these items should be available at pet supply stores or through a pet supply mail-order catalogs.

PUPPY ESSENTIALS

Your new puppy will need:

food bowl	bed
water bowl	crate
collar	toys
leash	grooming supplies
ID tag	

Collars

The rolled (or round leather) collar or a flat nylon collar with a buckle are great for Labs. Do not use a choke collar—they can be very dangerous, as the name implies, and should be used judiciously. A young Labrador can easily be taught to walk beside you without your using a choke collar.

Identification

Attach an identification tag with your address and telephone number to the collar. Add your Lab's rabies tag after she has had her rabies shot.

Many veterinarians offer tattooing or can tell you where this service is available. A dog is not usually tattooed until fully grown. You can

The best puppy to take home is one that looks healthy and happy and that is energetic and friendly.

have your dogs tattooed with your social security number and registered with the National Registry for a small fee.

Another option for identification is to have your veterinarian implant a chip the size of a grain of rice into your dog with the dog's pertinent information. Most veterinary hospitals, town pounds and shelter facilities now have scanners for these chips.

Leashes

You'll need a leash when your puppy is about 3 months old. A 4-foot-nylon or cotton-webbed leash is recommended to use for walks when you start leash training.

Flexi-leads are great for older trained dogs when you want to take them to a park or an exercise area

Throw a few toys into the shopping cart when you're out buying supplies.

11

Young puppies are curious creatures, so you'll want to prevent an accident before it happens by keeping household dangers out of reach.

and let them run without letting them off-lead.

IDENTIFY YOUR DOG

It is a terrible thing to think about, but your dog could somehow, someday, get lost or stolen. How would you get her back? Your best bet would be to have some form of identification on your dog. You can choose from a collar and tags, a tattoo, a microchip or a combination of these three.

Every dog should wear a buckle collar with identification tags. They are the quickest and easiest way for a stranger to identify your dog. It's best to inscribe the tags with your name and phone number; you should not include your dog's name.

There are two ways to permanently identify your dog. The first is a tattoo, placed on the inside of your dog's thigh. The tattoo should be your social security number or your dog's AKC registration number.

The second is a microchip, a rice-sized pellet that is inserted under the dog's skin at the base of the neck, between the shoulder blades. When a scanner is passed over the dog, it will beep, notifying the person that the dog has a chip. The scanner will then show a code, identifying the dog. Microchips are becoming more and more popular and are certainly the wave of the future.

Bowls

You'll need to get one bowl for food and one for water. Buying two 3-quart stainless-steel bowls is recommended. Labradors tend to make chew toys out of plastic bowls.

Crates

A crate is an excellent tool to use for housetraining and traveling. Dogs instinctively like to have a little den of their own. The crate provides that little den that they seek. The airline type of crate (rigid plastic box with ventilation holes) is the best crate for housetraining and car travel. It's more like a little dog house. A more open wire crate can be used for crating and traveling in warm weather.

When you bring home your new puppy, set up the crate in your bedroom. Your Lab will feel safe and secure knowing you are there, but she'll be confined and unable to do damage to your room or to herself. If the puppy uses the crate for sleeping at night, she will housetrain more quickly. She won't want to soil her sleeping quarters. When you go out, she'll be safe from eating or getting into something dangerous or expensive. During the daytime, pups should not be left in the crate for

Collars and leashes intended for puppies are smaller and made from softer materials than are those made for their adult counterparts.

over one hour at a time without the opportunity to eliminate. As the pup gets older and her baldder capacity increases, she may be left in the crate for longer periods of time.

When your Labrador is fully grown and totally reliable and trustworthy off-leash in the house (usually about 10 to 14 months old, depending on the dog and your training), let her sleep out of her crate. At this time, you can provide her with stuffed cedar beds or washable sheepskin (fake lambskin) rugs.

Exercise Pens

An exercise pen that is 3 or 4 feet high and 6 or 8 feet wide gives you another safe place to put your puppy

if she has to be left unsupervised a while. A pen isn't a replacement for a crate but is to be used in conjunction with a crate—in the yard or for traveling.

If you have two puppies, you may want to consider getting two crates.

CHAPTER THREE

To Good Health

the upkeep of a dog's health in relation to the calendar. Certain things need to be done on a weekly, monthly and annual basis.

PREVENTIVE HEALTH CARE

Weekly grooming can be the single best monitor of a dog's overall health. The actual condition of the coat and skin and the "feel" of the body can indicate good health or potential problems. Grooming will help you discover small lumps on or under the skin in the early stages before they become large enough to be seen without close examination.

You may spot fleas and ticks when brushing the coat and

The strongest body and soundest genetic background will not help a dog lead a healthy life unless he receives regular attention from his owner. Dogs are susceptible to infections, parasites and diseases for which they have no natural immunity. It is up to us to take preventative measures to make sure that none of these interferes with our dogs' health. It may help to think of examining the skin. Besides harboring diseases and parasites, they can make daily life a nightmare for some dogs. Dogs scratch, chew and destroy their coat and skin because of fleas. Even if the fleas are not actually seen, their existence can be confirmed by small black specks in the coat.

Flea Control

Flea control is never a simple endeavor. Dogs bring fleas inside, where they lay eggs in the carpeting and furniture—anywhere your dog goes in the house. Consequently, real control is a matter of not only treating the dog but also the other environments the flea inhabits. The yard can be sprayed, and in the house, sprays and flea bombs can be used, but there are more choices for the dog. Flea sprays are effective for one to two weeks depending on their ingredients. Dips applied to the dog's coat following a bath have equal periods of effectiveness. The disadvantage to both of these is that some dogs may have problems with the chemicals.

Flea collars can be effective, as they prevent the fleas from traveling to your dog's head, where it's moist

Run your hands regularly over your dog to feel for any injuries.

FIGHTING FLEAS

Remember, the fleas you see on your dog are only part of the problem—the smallest part! To rid your dog and home of fleas, you need to treat your dog and your home. Here's how:

- Identify where your pet(s) sleep. These are "hot spots."

- Clean your pets' bedding, your own floors and furniture regularly by vacuuming and washing.

- Spray "hot spots" with a nontoxic, long-lasting flea larvicide.

- Treat outdoor "hot spots" with insecticide.

- Kill eggs on pets with a product containing insect growth regulators (IGRs).

- Kill fleas on pets per your veterinarian's recommendation.

The flea is a die-hard pest.

and more hospitable. Dog owners tend to leave flea collars on their dogs long after they've ceased to be effective. Again, some dogs may have problems with flea collars, and children should never be allowed to handle them.

Some owners opt for a product that can work from the inside out. Veterinarians can apply a chemical to a spot on your dog's coat. The chemical is absorbed into the dog's body and works for up to a month. Another such option is a pill (prescribed by a veterinarian) that you give to the dog on a regular basis in his food. The chemicals in the pill course through the dog's bloodstream, and when a flea bites, the blood kills the flea.

Ticks

As you examine your dog, check also for ticks that may have lodged in his skin, particularly around the ears or in the hair at the base of the ear, the armpits or around the genitals. If you find a tick, which is a small insect about the size of a pencil eraser when engorged with blood, smear it thoroughly with petroleum jelly. As the tick suffocates in the petroleum jelly, it will back out and you can then grab it with tweezers and kill it. If the tick doesn't back out, grab it with tweezers and slowly pull it out, twisting very gently. Don't just grab and pull or the tick's head may separate from the body. If the head remains in the skin, an infection or abscess may result and veterinary treatment may be required.

A word of caution: Don't use your fingers or fingernails to pull out ticks. Ticks can carry a number of diseases, including Lyme disease, Rocky Mountain spotted fever and others, all of which can be very serious.

Proper Ear Care

Another weekly job is cleaning the ears. The moist environment created by ears that hang over the opening is a favorite place for infections to incubate.

Three types of ticks (l-r): the wood tick, brown dog tick and deer tick.

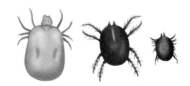

Many times an ear problem is evident if a dog scratches his ears or shakes his head frequently. Clean ears are less likely to develop problems, and if something does occur, it will be spotted while it can be treated easily. If a dog's ears are very dirty and seem to need cleaning on a daily basis, it is a good indication that something else is going on in the ears besides ordinary dirt and the normal accumulation of earwax. A visit to the veterinarian may indicate a situation that needs special medication.

Brushing Teeth

Regular brushing of the teeth often does not seem necessary when a dog is young and spends much of his time chewing; the teeth always seem to be immaculately clean. As a dog ages, it becomes more important to brush the teeth daily.

To help prolong the health of your dog's mouth, he should have his teeth cleaned twice a year at a veterinary clinic. Observing the mouth regularly, checking for the formation of abnormalities or broken teeth, can lead to early detection of oral cancer or infection.

Use tweezers to remove ticks from your dog.

Keeping Nails Trimmed

The nails on all feet should be kept short enough so they do not touch the ground when the dog walks.

Dogs with long nails can have difficulty walking on hard or slick surfaces. This can be especially true of older dogs. As nails grow longer, the toes themselves spread apart, causing the foot to become flattened and splayed.

Nails that are allowed to become long are also more prone to

Check your dog's teeth frequently and brush them regularly.

A healthy diet is essential to maintaining your dog's good health.

against the eye itself often exhibit more tearing than normal due to the irritation to the eyes. These eyelashes can be surgically removed if it appears to be a problem.

Excessive tearing can be an indication that a tear duct is blocked. This, too, can be corrected by a simple surgical procedure. Eye discharge that is thicker and mucous-like in consistency is often a sign of some type of eye infection or actual injury to the eye. This should be checked by a veterinarian.

VACCINES

All dogs need yearly vaccinations to protect them from common deadly diseases. The DHL vaccine, which protects a dog from distemper, hepatitis and leptospirosis, is given for the first time at about 7 weeks of age, followed by one or two boosters several weeks apart. After this, a dog should be vaccinated every year throughout his life.

Kennel cough, though rarely dangerous in a healthy dog that receives proper treatment, can be annoying. It can be picked up anywhere that large numbers of dogs congregate, such as veterinary clinics, grooming shops, boarding

splitting. This is painful to the dog and usually requires surgical removal of the remainder of the nail for proper healing to occur.

Keeping Eyes Clear

A Lab's eyes rarely need special attention. A small amount of matter in the corner of the eye is normal, as is a bit of "tearing." Dogs with eyelashes that turn inward and rub kennels, obedience classes and dog shows. The Bordatella vaccine, given twice a year, will protect a dog from getting most strains of kennel cough. It is often not routinely given, so it may be necessary to request it.

INTERNAL PARASITES

While the exterior part of a dog's body hosts fleas and ticks, the inside of the body is commonly inhabited by a variety of parasites. Most of these are in the worm family. Tapeworms, roundworms, whipworms, hookworms and heartworm all plague our canine friends. There are also several types of protozoa, mainly *coccidia* and *giardia,* that cause problems.

The common tapeworm is acquired by the dog eating infected fleas or lice. Normally one is not aware that a healthy dog even has tapeworms. The only clues may be a dull coat, a loss of weight despite a good appetite or occasional gastrointestinal problems. Confirmation is by the presence of worm segments in the stool. These appear as small, pinkish-white, flattened rectangular-shaped pieces. When dry, they look like rice. If segments are not present, diagnosis can be made by the discovery of eggs when a stool sample is examined under a microscope. Ridding a dog temporarily of tapeworm is easy with a worming medicine prescribed by a veterinarian. Over-the-counter wormers are not effective for tapeworms and may be dangerous. Long-term tapeworm control is not possible unless the flea situation is also handled.

Ascarids are the most common roundworm (nematode) found in dogs. Adult dogs that have roundworms rarely exhibit any symptoms that would indicate the worm is in their body. These worms are cylindrical in shape and may be as long as 4 to 5 inches. They do pose a real

YOUR PUPPY'S VACCINES

Vaccines are given to prevent your dog from getting an infectious disease like canine distemper or rabies. Vaccines are the ultimate preventive medicine. That's why it is necessary for your dog to be vaccinated routinely. Puppy vaccines start at 8 weeks of age for the five-in-one DHLPP vaccine. Your veterinarian will put your puppy on a proper schedule and should remind you when to bring in your dog for shots.

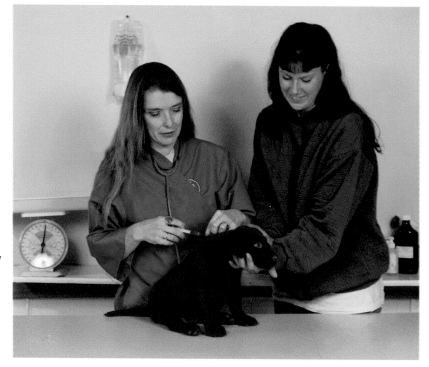

Vaccinations will help protect your dog from the most common infectious canine diseases.

danger to puppies, where they are usually passed from the mother through the uterus to the unborn puppies.

It is wise to assume that all puppies have roundworms. In heavy infestations they will actually appear in the puppy stools, though their presence is best diagnosed by a stool sample. Treatment is easy and can begin as early as 2 weeks of age and is administered every two weeks thereafter until eggs no longer appear in a stool sample or dead worms are not found in the stool following treatment. Severely infected puppies can die from roundworm infestation. Again, the worming medication should be obtained through a veterinarian.

Hookworm is usually found in warmer climates and infestation is generally from ingestion of larvae from the ground or penetration of the skin by larvae. Hookworms can cause anemia, diarrhea and emaciation. As these worms are very tiny and not visible to the eye, their diagnosis must be made by a veterinarian.

Whipworms live in the large intestine and cause few if any symptoms. Dogs usually become infected when they ingest larvae in contaminated soil. Again, diagnosis and treatment should all be done by a veterinarian. One of the easiest ways to control these parasites is by picking up stools on a daily basis. This will help prevent the soil from becoming infested.

The protozoa can be trickier to diagnose and treat. Coccidiosis and giardia are the most common and primarily affect young puppies. They are generally associated with overcrowded, unsanitary conditions and can be acquired from the mother (if she is a carrier), the premises themselves (soil) or even water, especially rural puddles and streams.

The most common symptom of protozoan infection is mucous-like blood-tinged feces. It is only with freshly collected samples that diagnosis of this condition can be made. With coccidiosis, besides diarrhea, the puppies will appear listless and lose their appetites. Puppies often harbor the protozoa and show no symptoms unless placed under stress. Consequently, many times a

puppy will not become ill until he goes to his new home. Once diagnosed, treatment is quick and effective, and the puppy returns to normal almost immediately.

Heartworm

The most serious of the common internal parasites is the heartworm. A dog that is bitten by a mosquito infected with the heartworm *microfilaria* (larvae) will develop worms that are 6 to 12 inches long. As these worms mature they take up residence in the dog's heart.

The symptoms of heartworm may include coughing, tiring easily, difficulty breathing and weight loss. Heart failure and liver disease may eventually result. Verification of heartworm infection is done by drawing blood and screening for the microfilaria.

In areas where heartworm is a risk, it is best to place a dog on a preventative, usually a pill given

21

Common internal parasites (l-r): roundworm, whipworm, tapeworm and hookworm.

once a month. Because the mosquitoes require warm temperatures to propagate, concern for heartworm transmission is limited to the warmer months of the year. Consequently, many owners only give their dogs heartworm preventative for a portion of the year. Anytime a dog is taken off heartworm preventative and then placed back on it, he must have his blood checked to make sure he is not harboring heartworm.

At least once a year a dog should have a full veterinary examination. The overall condition of the dog can be observed and a blood sample collected for a complete yearly screening. This way the dog's thyroid functions can be tested, and the job the dog's organs are doing can be monitored. If there are any problems, this form of testing can spot trouble areas while they are easily treatable.

Proper care, regular vaccinations, periodic stool checks and preventative medications for such things as heartworm will all help ensure your dog's health.

SPAYING/NEUTERING

Spaying a female dog or neutering a male is another way to make sure they lead long and healthy lives.

22

Depending on what part of the country you live in, and on the severity of that area's mosquito infestation, your vet may recommend giving your dog a monthly heartworm preventative.

Females spayed at a young age have almost no risk of developing mammary tumors or reproductive problems. Neutering a male is an excellent solution to dog aggression and also removes the chances of testicular cancer.

There is absolutely no benefit to a female having a first season before being spayed, nor in letting her have a litter. The decision to breed any dog should never be taken lightly. The obvious considerations are whether he or she is a good physical specimen of the breed and has a sound temperament. There are several genetic problems that are common to Labs, such as progressive retinal atrophy (PRA), retinal dysplasia, cataracts, hip dysplasia, osteochondrosis (damage to joint cartilage) and lameness. Responsible breeders screen for these prior to making breeding decisions.

Finding suitable homes for puppies is another serious consideration. Due to their popularity, many people are attracted to Labs and seek puppies without realizing the drawbacks of the breed.

Owning a dog is a lifetime commitment to that animal. There are so many unwanted dogs—and yes,

ADVANTAGE OF SPAYING/NEUTERING

The greatest advantage of spaying (for females) or neutering (for males) your dog is that you are guaranteed that your dog will not produce puppies. There are too many puppies already available for too few homes. There are other advantages as well.

Advantages of Spaying

No messy heats.

No "suitors" howling at your windows or waiting in your yard.

Prevents pyometra (disease of the uterus) and decreases the incidence of breast cancer.

Advantages of Neutering

Decreases fights, but doesn't affect the dog's personality.

Decreases roaming.

Decreased incidences of urogenital diseases.

even unwanted Labs—that people must be absolutely sure that they are not just adding to the pet overpopulation problem. When breeding a litter of puppies, it is more likely that you will lose more than you will make, when time, effort, equipment and veterinary costs are factored in.

COMMON PROBLEMS

Lameness

A limp that appears from nowhere and gets progressively worse is cause for concern. The first thing to do is try to ascertain where the problem actually is. Check the legs and feet for any areas of tenderness, swelling or infection. There are numerous possibilities to consider. In young, developing dogs, lameness in the rear can be an indication of hip dysplasia.

Hip dysplasia is a malformation of the ball and socket joint of the hips and can affect one or both sides of the dog. As a dog ages these joints wear down, and eventually arthritis is associated with the disease. Hip dysplasia can only be properly diagnosed by x-ray.

If x-rays do confirm hip dysplasia, there are several considerations. Surgery is one alternative in more serious cases. In very serious cases the hips themselves are removed and may be replaced with Teflon hips. Most mildly and many moderately dysplastic dogs will lead normal lives if properly managed. A dysplastic dog should be kept in good weight and physical condition. Moderate

exercise, especially swimming, is necessary if a dysplastic dog is to lead a normal life. If pain develops with age, it can be relieved with aspirin.

Another common condition that causes lameness in young dogs is osteochondritis dissecans (OCD). This disease affects the shoulder joints and sometimes the hocks and stifles. OCD can be confirmed by x-ray, and the cartilage appears fragmented or loose. In mild cases it will heal itself with rest but usually requires surgery.

Another serious concern with lameness, especially as a dog ages, is bone cancer. This can only be confirmed by tests and x-rays. Anytime a dog or puppy becomes lame and rest is prescribed as treatment, it is essential to keep that dog almost completely inactive, except for potty visits, until the injury heals.

Not Eating or Vomiting

One of the surest signs that a Labrador Retriever may be ill is if he does not eat. This is why it is important to know your dog's eating habits. For most dogs one missed meal under normal conditions is not cause for alarm, but more than that and it is time to take your dog to the veterinarian to search for reasons. The vital signs should be checked and gums examined. Normally a dog's gums are pink; if ill they will be pale and gray.

There are many reasons why dogs vomit, and many of them are not cause for alarm. If they eat too much grass they vomit. If they drink too much water too fast they often vomit. You should be concerned, however, when your dog vomits frequently over the period of a day. If the vomiting is associated with diarrhea, elevated temperature and lethargy, the cause is most likely a virus. The dog should receive supportive veterinary treatment if recovery is to proceed quickly. Vomiting that is not associated with other symptoms is often an indication of an intestinal blockage. Rocks, toys and clothing will lodge in a dog's intestine, preventing the normal passage of digested foods and liquids.

If a blockage is suspected, the first thing to do is x-ray the stomach and intestinal region. Sometimes objects will pass on their own, but usually surgical removal of the object is necessary.

Diarrhea

Diarrhea is characterized as very loose to watery stools that a dog has difficulty controlling. It can be caused by anything as simple as changing diet, eating too much food, eating rich human food or having internal parasites.

First try to locate the source of the problem and remove it from the dog's access. Immediate relief is

WHEN TO CALL THE VETERINARIAN

In any emergency situation, you should call your veterinarian immediately. You can make the difference in your dog's life by staying as calm as possible when you call and by giving the veterinarian or the assistant as much information as possible before you leave for the clinic. That way, the staff will be able to take immediate, specific action to remedy your dog's situation.

Emergencies include acute abdominal pain, suspected poisoning, snakebite, burns, frostbite, shock, dehydration, abnormal vomiting or bleeding and deep wounds. You are the best judge of your dog's health, as you live with and observe him every day. Don't hesitate to call your veterinarian if you suspect trouble.

usually available by giving the dog an intestinal relief medication such as Kaopectate or Pepto-Bismol. Use the same amount per weight as for humans. Take the dog off his food for a day to allow the intestines to rest, then feed meals of cooked rice with bland ingredients added. Gradually add the dog's regular food back into his diet.

If the diarrhea is bloody or has a more offensive odor than might be expected and is combined with vomiting and fever, it is most likely a virus and requires immediate veterinary attention. If worms are suspected as the cause, a stool sample should be examined by a veterinarian and treatment to rid the dog of the parasite should follow when the dog is back to normal. If allergies are suspected, a series of tests can be given to find the cause. This is especially likely if, after recovery and no other evidence of a cause exists, a dog returns to his former diet and the diarrhea recurs.

Bloat

Another problem associated with the gastrointestinal system is bloat, or acute gastric dilatation. It most commonly occurs in adult dogs that eat large amounts of dry kibble. Exercise or excessive amounts of water consumed immediately following a meal can trigger the condition.

A dog with bloat will appear restless and uncomfortable. He may drool and attempt to vomit. The abdominal area will appear swollen, and the area will be painful. In severe cases, the stomach actually twists on itself and a condition called torsion occurs. If you suspect that your dog is suffering from bloat, take him to the nearest veterinary clinic immediately.

Bloat can be prevented by feeding smaller amounts of food several times per day rather than in one large meal. Soaking the food in water prior to feeding it will also help reduce the risk of bloat. Additionally, the dog should be kept from exercising until two or three hours after eating.

Seizures

Seizures vary in severity from trembling and stiffness to frenzied, rapid movements of the legs, foaming at the mouth and loss of urine and bowel movements. The latter is usually considered a grand mal seizure.

Seizures are caused by electrical activity in the brain, and there are many reasons why they may occur. Ingestion of some poisons, such as strychnine and insecticides, will cause seizures. These are generally long lasting and severe in nature. Injuries to the skull, tumors and cancers can trigger seizures.

If there appears to be no reason for the seizure, it is possible the cause is congenital epilepsy. This is particularly true if a dog is under the age of 3. From the age of 5, dogs are prone to develop old age onset epilepsy, which also may have a genetic predisposition.

Never try to touch or move a dog during a seizure. If there is anything nearby that might be knocked over by their flailing legs and injure them, move it out of the way. If the seizure does not stop within five minutes, call your veterinarian.

Even after a typical seizure, your vet may suggest that you bring your dog in for an examination and blood work. If a cause is not found, the best course is usually to wait and see if your dog has another seizure. If a dog only has seizures once or twice a year, there is no reason to place him on preventive medication. If seizures occur on a regular basis and are of

the same nature each time, the dog is considered to have epilepsy and medication should be considered.

In typical epilepsy, the dog may act restless, weird, stare and bark for some time before the actual seizure. The seizure itself lasts several minutes. A second seizure can be triggered by turning a light on or by moving the dog as he is recovering.

If seizures are infrequent and mild, an epileptic dog can lead a fairly normal life. Owners will generally begin to see a pattern in the time of day the seizures occur and their frequency, and can plan their dog's activities accordingly.

Coughing

Throughout the day, most dogs will cough to get something out of their throats, and it is usually ignored. If coughing persists, then it is time to look for causes.

A common cause for a dry hacking cough is kennel cough, which is contagious and usually picked up through association with other dogs. A dog with kennel cough should receive veterinary attention and be placed on antibiotics and a cough suppressant. During treatment and recovery, the dog should be kept

Applying abdominal thrusts can save a choking dog.

indoors and warm as much as possible. Kennel cough, if not cared for properly, can easily turn into pneumonia in cold conditions. Infected dogs should be isolated from other dogs until they have recovered.

Chronic coughing after exercise can also be a sign of heart failure, especially in an older dog. It may also indicate a heartworm infection. If this occurs regularly, consult your veterinarian.

Most changes in the breathing pattern of a healthy dog, such as rapid inhalations or panting, are caused by exercise, stress and heat. If a dog is having problems breathing and it is also accompanied by coughing or gagging, it may be a sign that an air passage is blocked. Check for an object lodged in your dog's throat. If you can't remove it yourself, use the Heimlich maneuver. Place your dog on his side and, using both hands palms down, apply quick thrusts to the abdomen, just below the dog's last rib. If your dog

won't lie down, grasp either side of the end of the rib cage and squeeze in short thrusts. Make a sharp enough movement to cause the air in the lungs to force the object out. If the cause cannot be found or removed, then professional help is needed.

Shallow breathing can be a result of an injury to the ribs or a lung problem. A wheezing noise that can be heard as a dog breathes is an indication of a serious problem. If other symptoms include a fever and lethargy, the problem may be associated with a lung disease. The symptoms may indicate treatment for an infection. An x-ray can confirm the presence of a growth or infection in the lungs.

Sometimes a dog exhibits no greater signs that something is different than increased lethargy, weight gain and even a poor coat. It may be time to consider checking the dog's thyroid levels for a possible hypothyroid condition. Low thyroid most commonly results in a poor coat and skin and eventual infertility in an intact male or female. A thyroid test will indicate what levels of the function of the thyroid are low and whether daily thyroid medication should be given.

Skin Problems

Certain skin conditions should not be ignored if home treatment is not working. For example, if a dog is so sensitive and allergic to fleas that his coat and skin are literally destroyed by chewing, it is time to seek help. Cortisone can help relieve the itching and stop the dog from destroying himself, but it has side effects, too! It's best to get your vet's advice.

Mange is caused by tiny mites that live on the dog's skin. The most common types are sarcoptic and demodetic mange. Diagnosis must be made by a veterinarian because the mites are too small to be seen.

Sarcoptic mange first occurs as small red bumps on the dog's skin and causes intense itching. If allowed to continue, there is hair loss from chewing, and the affected skin becomes crusty, especially around the muzzle, elbows and hocks.

The mite that causes demodetic mange lives in the pores of the skin of most dogs. Certain conditions cause the dog's natural immunity to this mite to break down, and the result is patches of hair loss, usually around the nose or eyes. There is no itching associated with this condition, and it primarily occurs in dogs under 1 year of age. If treated properly the hair returns to normal. In the generalized form of the disease, hair loss occurs in large patches all over the body. Obviously this is a much more serious condition.

Hot spots are one of the most baffling skin problems. They can be caused by a number of things, including flea bites and allergies. A warm, moist, infected area on the skin appears out of nowhere and can be several inches large. At home one should clip the hair around it, then clean it with an antiseptic and dilute (3 percent hydrogen peroxide). Spraying with a topical anaesthetic immediately relieves itching. Topical ointments can also help. If the spot is not healing and appears to be getting larger or infected, veterinary help should be sought.

A similar type of skin condition is the lick sore. These sores are almost always on the lower part of the front legs or tops of the feet. A dog will lick a spot and out of boredom continue licking it until the hair is gone and the skin is hard, red and shiny. The sore will heal on its own if kept clean and the dog is prevented access to it by an anti-

29

*An Elizabethan
collar keeps your
dog from licking
a fresh wound.*

chewing spray or by wearing an
Elizabethan collar.

Tumors

As dogs age they are more apt to
develop various types of tumors.
Fatty tumors grow just under the
dog's skin and are not attached to
anything. These are usually benign
accumulations of fatty cells. If you
see or feel any such lumps on your
dog, you should consult your veterinarian. Tumors and bumps that
appear and grow rapidly, are strange
in color or appearance or are
attached to the bone should receive
immediate attention.

Cuts and Wounds

Any cut over $1/2$ inch in length
should be stitched for it to heal.
Small cuts usually heal by themselves if they are rinsed well, washed

with an antibiotic soap and checked
regularly with further cleansing of
soap or a hydrogen peroxide solution. When they occur in areas that
are exposed to dirt, such as the feet,
it may be advisable to place a wrap
on the injury, but it should be
removed frequently. If signs of infection appear, such as swelling, redness
or warmth, it should be looked at by
a veterinarian.

Puncture wounds should never
be bandaged or stitched. They occur
most commonly from bites, nails or
wires. Anytime it is suspected that a
dog might have been pierced by a
nail or bitten, the body should be
carefully examined for such wounds.
As they often do not bleed very
much, they can be difficult to spot.
If not treated, they can result in
infection or even conditions as dangerous as tetanus.

If the wound is discovered within a short time of the occurrence, try
to make it bleed by applying pressure around it. Flush it with water,
then clean it with soap. Leave it
exposed so that oxygen is able to
stay in the wound and prevent an
anaerobic condition from developing. Place a dilute hydrogen peroxide on it several times a day. Watch
it carefully for any indications of

infection. Anytime your dog is injured, consider placing him on an antibiotic to prevent infection.

To give a pill, open the mouth wide, then drop it in the back of the throat.

GIVING MEDICATION

When a dog has been diagnosed with a problem that requires medication, it is usually in the form of a pill or liquid. Because it is essential for a dog to have the entire pill or capsule in order for the dosage to be effective, it's necessary to actually give the dog the pill rather than mix it in his food or wrap it in meat, which can be chewed up and spit out. Open your dog's mouth and place the pill on the back of the middle of his tongue. Then hold his head up with his mouth held shut and stroke his throat. When the dog swallows, you can let go.

Liquid medication is most easily given in a syringe. These are usually marked so the amount is accurately measured. Hold the dog's head upward at about 45°, open the mouth slightly and place the end of the syringe in the area in the back of the mouth between the cheek and rear molars. Hold your dog's mouth shut until he swallows.

If your dog needs eye medication, apply it by pulling down the lower eyelid and placing the ointment on the inside of the lid. Then close the eye and gently disperse the solution around the eye. Eye drops can be placed directly on the eye. Giving ear medicine is similar to cleaning the ears. The drops are placed in the canal and the ear is then massaged.

COMMON LABRADOR RETRIEVER PROBLEMS

CATARACTS—There are several types of cataracts that affect Labs. They are characterized by the part of the lens on which they appear and the age of the dog. Most are genetic, though others can be caused

Squeeze eye ointment into the lower lid.

31

of the cartilage of the long bones that subsequently results in the injury of that cartilage. This can be treated by rest in minor cases or surgery. X-rays verify this condition.

PROGRESSIVE RETINAL ATROPHY (PRA)—PRA is a gradual degeneration of the cells of the retina. It first occurs in middle-aged dogs and leads to loss of vision. Diagnosis is the same as for cataracts. CERF (Canine Eye Registry Foundation) was established to benefit breeding programs by registering dogs whose eyes test free of genetic problems.

FIRST AID AND EMERGENCIES

While we never plan on emergencies happening, we can be partially prepared by knowing which veterinary clinics are open if something occurs at night or on the weekend. Telephone numbers should be posted so they can be easily located. First-aid measures can be taken to help ensure that your dog gets to a veterinarian in time for treatment to be effective.

Anytime a dog is in extreme pain, even the most docile one may

While neither could be detected in a puppy this young, cataracts and PRA are two eye problems that are common in Labradors and which you and your vet should keep an eye out for as your dog ages.

by injury or the aging process. Most cataracts are nonprogressive in Labs, and impairment of vision is usually mild. Diagnosis must be made by a veterinary ophthalmologist.

HIP DYSPLASIA—Genetic and environmental in origin, it is the malformation of the ball and socket joints of the hips. Severe forms cause lameness and may require surgery. Diagnosis is only by x-ray.

OSTEOCHONDRITIS DISSECANS (OCD)—There appears to be a genetic predisposition to malformation bite if touched. As a precaution, the dog's mouth should be restrained with some type of muzzle. A rope, pair of pantyhose or strip of cloth about 2 feet long all work in a pinch.

First tie a loose knot that has an opening large enough to easily fit around the dog's nose. Once it is on, tighten the knot on the top of the muzzle. Then bring the two ends down and tie another knot underneath the dog's chin. Finally, pull the ends behind the head and tie a knot below the ears. Don't do this if there is an injury to the head or the dog requires artificial respiration.

If a dog has been injured or is too ill to walk on his own, he will have to be carried to be moved. It is important to be very careful when this is done to prevent further injury or trauma. Keep the dog's body as flat and still as possible. Two people are usually needed to move a large dog. A blanket can work if all four corners are held taut. A piece of plywood or extremely stiff cardboard works best, if available.

ARTIFICIAL RESPIRATION—

Artificial respiration is necessary if breathing has stopped. Situations that may cause a state of unconsciousness include drowning, choking, electric shock or even shock itself. If you've taken a course in human CPR, you will discover that

33

It is possible to detect whether your dog will be prone to hip dysplasia through x-rays.

A First-Aid Kit

Keep a canine first-aid kit on hand for general care and emergencies. Check it periodically to make sure liquids haven't spilled or dried up, and replace medications and materials after they're used. Your kit should include:

- Activated charcoal tablets
- Adhesive tape (1 and 2 inches wide)
- Antibacterial ointment (for skin and eyes)
- Aspirin (buffered or enteric coated, not ibuprofen or acetaminophen)
- Bandages: gauze rolls (1 and 2 inches wide) and dressing pads
- Cotton balls
- Diarrhea medicine
- Dosing syringe
- Hydrogen peroxide (3%)
- Petroleum jelly
- Rectal thermometer
- Rubber gloves
- Rubbing alcohol
- Scissors
- Tourniquet
- Towel
- Tweezers

similar methods are used on dogs. The first thing to do is check the mouth and air passages for any object that might obstruct breathing. If you find nothing, or when it is cleared, hold the dog's mouth while covering the nose completely with your mouth. Gently exhale into the dog's nose. This should be done at between ten to twelve breaths per minute.

If the heart has stopped beating, place the dog on his right side and place the palm of your hand on the rib cage just behind the elbows. Press down six times and then wait five seconds and repeat. This should be done in conjunction with artificial respiration, so it will require two people. Artificial respiration should be continued until the dog breathes on his own or the heart beats. Heart massage should continue until the heart beats on its own or no beat is felt for five minutes.

SHOCK—Whenever a dog is injured or is seriously ill, the odds are good that he will go into a state of shock. A dog in shock will be listless, weak and cold to the touch. His gums will be pale. If not treated, a dog will die from shock, even if

Use a scarf or old hose to make a temporary muzzle, as shown.

the illness or injuries themselves are not fatal. The conditions of the dog should continue to be treated, but the dog should be kept as comfortable as possible. A blanket can help keep the dog warm. A dog in shock needs immediate veterinary care.

SEVERE BLEEDING—When severe bleeding from a cut occurs, the area should be covered with bandaging material or a clean cloth and should have pressure applied to it. If it appears that an artery is involved and the wound is on a limb, then a tourniquet should be applied. This can be made of a piece of cloth, gauze or sock if nothing else is available. It should be tied above the wound and checked every few minutes to make sure it is not so tight that circulation to the rest of the limb is cut off.

FRACTURES—If a fracture is felt or suspected, the dog should be moved and transported as carefully as possible to a veterinarian. Attempting to treat a break at home can cause more damage than leaving it alone.

POISONING—In the case of poisoning the only thing to do is get help immediately. If you know the source of the poison, take the container or object with you, as this may aid treatment.

In acidic or alkaline poisonings the chemicals must be neutralized. Pepto-Bismol or milk of magnesia at 2 teaspoons per 5 pounds of weight can be given for acids.

Some of the many household substances harmful to your dog.

Vinegar diluted at one part to four parts water at the same dosage can relieve alkaline poisons.

HEATSTROKE—Heatstroke occurs when a dog's body temperature greatly exceeds the normal 101.5°F. It can be caused by overexercise in warm temperatures or if a dog is left in a closed vehicle for any period of time. A dog should *never* be left in an unventilated, unshaded vehicle. Even if you only plan to be gone for a minute, that time can unexpectedly increase and place a dog in a life-threatening situation.

Dogs suffering from heatstroke will feel hot to the touch and inhale short, shallow, rapid breaths. The heartbeat will be very fast. The dog must be cooled immediately, preferably being wet down with cool water in any way that is available. The dog should be wrapped in cool, damp towels. Shock is another possible side effect of heatstroke. The dog should also receive veterinary care. Even

when a dog survives heatstroke, permanent brain damage may occur.

The opposite of heatstroke is hypothermia. When a dog is exposed to extreme cold for long periods of time, his body temperature drops, he becomes chilled and he can go into shock. The dog should be placed in a warm environment and wrapped in towels or blankets. If the dog is already wet, a warm bath can help. Massaging the body will help increase the circulation to normal levels.

INSECT BITES —The seriousness of reactions to insect bites varies. The affected area will be red, swollen and painful. In the case of bee stings the stinger should always be removed. A paste made of baking soda and water can be applied to the wound and ice applied to the area for the relief of swelling. The bites of some spiders, centipedes and scorpions can cause severe illness and lead to shock.

CHAPTER FOUR

Positively Nutritious

Every dog needs to be fed appropriately for her age and level of stress and exercise. Most quality foods come in puppy, adult, maintenance, high-test or performance for skin and coat problems and senior or light form.

WHEN TO FEED

A twice-a-day feeding plan is highly recommended for Labs. They are prone to destructive chewing, so just one feeding a day may not be enough activity for them. It's a well-known fact that Labradors like to eat. In fact, many dogs seem to be happier and less likely to get into trouble when they eat twice a day, or three times a day.

Young pups need to eat small amounts over a day. Pups' stomachs are small and cannot take in the amount of food they need for the whole day all at once. You know it's time to increase the amount of food if, when you put it down, your Lab gobbles it up and runs about looking

How Many Meals a Day?

Individual dogs vary in how much they should eat to maintain a desired body weight—not too fat, but not too thin. Puppies need several meals a day, while older dogs may only need one. Determine how much food keeps your adult dog looking and feeling her best, then decide how many meals you want to feed with that amount. Like us, most dogs love to eat, and offering two meals a day is more enjoyable for them. If you're worried about overfeeding, make sure you measure correctly and abstain from adding tidbits to the meals.

Whether you feed one or two meals, only leave your dog's food out for the amount of time it takes her to eat it—10 minutes, for example. Free-feeding (when food's available any time) and leisurely meals encourage picky eating. Don't worry if your dog doesn't finish all her dinner in the allotted time. She'll learn she should.

for more. You'll have to decrease the number of meals but increase the amount at each meal somewhere in that 3- to 4-month-old stage. Generally, dogs may be kept on puppy food until they are 6 to 8 months old. You and your veterinarian must decide when your Lab is ready to switch to adult food.

What to Feed

Basically, if you feed a good-quality food, your dog will be getting a balanced diet. Labrador Retrievers are usually good eaters, so it's easy for you to put down a well-balanced meal in one bowl. Avoid the gimmicky stuff that looks like meat or hamburgers or food that makes its own gravy. These types are loaded with preservatives and red dyes. It would be like giving your child hot dogs and candy as a steady diet just because that was what he or she liked. You wouldn't do it to your child, so don't do it to your Labrador.

Labs are known for their appetites, so it's rare that any food is left after feeding time. Make sure to note your Lab's normal eating habits. If you know what is normal, it's easier to notice when something is abnormal. If she goes off her food for two or more meals, she could be ill. You should take her temperature and have a look in her mouth to see if there is a tooth problem. Sometimes, dogs coming down with kennel cough or sore throats go off their feed. If the problem is a twenty-four-hour episode and her appetite returns to normal after a day, you have nothing to worry about. If she continues to refuse food and water, consult your veterinarian.

You should be careful of additives in dog foods. Cancer is on the rise in dogs, so it makes sense to take a good look at the ingredients and preservatives in the food. Cancer is another reason to avoid feeding your Lab junk food.

Many good dry foods are designed for every stage of your dog's life. There are also special formulas for dogs that have allergies, are overweight and so forth. You should select a dry variety that matches your dog's situation and make sure to try the food for at least a month. If your Lab is eating away, you have your food!

Inactive Labradors tend to put on excess weight very quickly. You must monitor and adjust food according to their activity level and nutritional needs. You must also remember that if you are giving between-meal treats such as biscuits, a couple of large biscuits add up to another $1/2$ cup or so of food. You must account for this when you are deciding how much food to feed your dog daily.

A Lab's frame should be well covered with coat as well as body substance. A lot of fat is not good for your dog. The right combination of diet and exercise will keep your dog at the proper weight. You must monitor the situation carefully month to month because her dietary needs can change from season to season as well as from year to year. If your Lab doesn't spend a lot of time outside in the winter running and expending calories, cut back on her rations. If she's often outside in the snow bounding through drifts, she may need a bit more food. Be

Puppies need to have several small meals over the course of a day.

HOW TO READ THE DOG FOOD LABEL

With so many choices on the market, how can you be sure you're feeding the right food for your dog? The information's all there on the label—if you know what you're looking for. Look for the nutritional claim right up top. Is the food "100% nutritionally complete"? If so, it's for nearly all life stages; "growth and maintenance," on the other hand, is for early development; puppy foods are marked as such, as are foods for senior dogs.

Ingredients are listed in descending order by weight. The first three or four ingredients will tell you the bulk of what the food contains. Look for the highest-quality ingredients, like meats and grains, to be among them.

The guaranteed analysis tells you what levels of protein, fat, fiber and moisture are in the food, in that order. While these numbers are meaningful, they won't tell you much about the quality of the food. Nutritional value is in the dry matter, not the moisture content.

In many ways, seeing is believing. If your dog has bright eyes, a shiny coat, a good appetite and a good energy level, chances are her diet's fine. Labrador Retrievers rarely skip their meals.

observant. It is believed that hip dysplasia and other orthopedic problems can be inherited, but they

can also be brought on or exacerbated by diet and lack of or too much exercise. Puppies need to be exercising on surfaces where they have good traction. During their developmental stages, if they are slipping and sliding and overweight to boot, don't be surprised if problems arise.

Supplements

If you want to supplement your dog's diet, you can give a multivitamin daily and 1,500 to 2,000 mg of vitamin C to dogs under stress. You might also consider giving about $1/4$ cup of plain yogurt with live cultures three times a week to your dog. A $1/4$-cup portion of scrambled eggs (just twice a week) is another nutritious supplement. Never feed raw eggs to dogs, only scrambled or boiled is recommended.

Aside from giving dogs a small amount of plain yogurt, avoid feeding them other dairy foods except for the occasional piece of cheese as a treat or reward. If you're feeding a good professional-quality food, your dog is getting enough fat and protein. Extra dairy, like a bowl of milk, may add too much fat and is likely to give your dog diarrhea.

At the Dinner Table

Dogs should be taught good behavior at mealtime, right from the start. Though a Labrador is more convenient than a dust buster for those stray crumbs, peas and so forth, never hand them food or give in to their begging at the table.

Labradors don't usually sit up and beg on their hind legs like some other dogs do. Labs are more apt to have their noses up to the table or in your lap. They will nose around between your legs and feet and will be annoying in general if they are not taught to lie down during dinner. It's all up to you. If you let your Lab think it's okay to nose around and beg, she will. If you teach her the Sit, Down and Stay commands and give the commands when you sit at the table, she will accept and obey.

Feeding from the table will skew your dog's routine. You may inadvertently feed her too much, and she may become overweight. Also, some foods can upset her stomach. You should never feed spicy or greasy foods, and you should be particularly cautious never to feed chocolate because it is poisonous to dogs.

A daily multi-vitamin and ¹/₄-cup of plain yogurt three times a week are acceptable ways to supplement your dog's diet.

41

POSSIBLE PROBLEMS

If your dog develops an allergy or skin problem, your veterinarian may recommend a prescription diet in a can or a dry food specifically formulated for skin problems. There is a prescription diet formulated for just about any problem your dog may have, including special diets for kidney, liver and intestinal problems. These diets are prescribed by your veterinarian after conclusive tests that show a problem with a specific organ or system.

Labradors, especially if they aren't very active, have a tendency to put on excess weight, a problem most effectively solved by a modest diet and regular exercise.

Try to find a food that seems to agree with your dog and stick with it unless problems arise or your dog's lifestyle changes drastically. The worst thing you can do is switch back and forth, trying this food and that, buying one brand this week because you have a coupon and another brand the following week. You'll be better off sticking to one brand unless your dog is not thriving on her diet. Try a new food for at least one month before you decide how she is doing on it. If, however, she has an allergic reaction or if the food causes vomiting, diarrhea or abstinence, reevaluate the situation sooner.

The moral of this story is buy a good food, feed it correctly, check stools yearly and your Labrador Retriever should thrive.

CHAPTER FIVE

Putting on the Dog

If you are a new Lab owner or about to become one, you will discover that they need only minimal coat care. The Labrador's natural coat is pretty much wash and wear. As a rule, Labs don't need much bathing. They have a natural oil to their coats, and too much bathing strips the coat of it.

The Labrador can withstand very cold water because of its double coat. He has a thick undercoat under a harsh-feeling topcoat. The texture of the coat differs from color to color.

SHEDDING

Females will usually shed out twice a year. Their hair growth and

A grooming mitt will help you keep your Lab's shedding under control, especially during the spring and fall shedding seasons.

shedding are a consequence of hormonal changes.

Males as well as spayed females usually have one big shed-out in the spring and a smaller hair loss in the autumn. Sometimes, coats get more harsh and profuse with age. Coat quality is largely a product of genetics, but the coat is also affected by climate, living conditions and diet.

BRUSHING

Begin with a good, strong nylon or natural bristle brush, once or twice a week on the coat. You can also roll up a rough towel and buff the coat.

Start up by your Lab's neck and pull the towel down toward the tail. Labradors love the attention that comes with grooming, and they usually cooperate.

Use a comb or slicker brush when it's time for the coat to come out and it's coming out by the handful when you touch your dog. If the coat is coming out anyway, try to help it along. The idea is to change the coat as quickly as possible. At this time, a few warm baths also help to speed the process. A warm bath with a mild shampoo followed by a rough toweling and then a combing or a brushing with a slicker brush will be a big help.

For general care, a good brushing a few times a week and a wipe and shine with a chamois cloth or towel will make your Lab's coat look just fine. It is, however, a good idea to buy a flea comb. This is a special comb with teeth so close together that the fleas and flea dirt are trapped, and you can comb them right off the dog and into a pan of alcohol.

If you come across a tick when you're brushing, you can use tweezers to pull it out. Make sure you pull out the head of the tick by pinching with the tweezers as close as possible to the body. Apply antiseptic to the bite site. Dispose of the tick carefully by dropping it from the tweezers into alcohol.

If your dog has a flea problem, adding garlic and brewer's yeast to his food is recommended. Flea collars, sprays, powders or dips are not recommended unless they are herbal.

All Labs can be bothered by fleas, but sometimes the light yellows have more sensitive skin. Some dogs are very allergic to fleas. There are many ways to treat fleas. You may consider systemic dog products, flea removal from the dog and regular cleansing and treatment of the dog's environment.

GROOMING TOOLS

pin brush	scissors
slicker brush	nail clippers
flea comb	tooth-cleaning
towel	equipment
matt rake	shampoo
grooming glove	conditioner
clippers	

45

A thorough brushing a few times a week and an occasional bath are about all the grooming a Lab's coat needs to stay in good shape.

TRIMMING THE NAILS

Your Labrador's nails should be trimmed so that you cannot hear them clicking on the floor. Besides large-size nail clippers, you should buy styptic powder specifically for

Labrador Retrievers' thick, water-resistant coats allow them to withstand very cold water temperatures.

dog nails. Start good nail care when your puppy is young so that he will become accustomed to the procedure. Make nail clipping a part of your grooming routine every ten days to two weeks. If your Lab has his dewclaws, always check to make sure they are kept short.

If your Lab goes for regular walks on pavement or runs back and forth on a cement dog run, the four front and rear nails will be fairly worn down, and you'll probably just need to clip the hook part of the nails. Most of the time a minor cut to the quick will stop bleeding on its own. The styptic powder will stop the bleeding; if it doesn't, applying the powder along with some pressure does the job.

The most important thing to remember when trimming your dog's nails is not to cut too much and nick the quick.

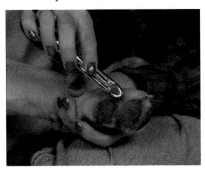

TEETH

A large dog biscuit once a day is good for your dog's teeth. In conjunction with his dry kibble, it will help keep his teeth clean. Chew toys can also help to keep tartar and plaque to a minimum.

As dogs get older, we can help counter the progression of tooth decay and gum disease by regularly brushing the teeth.

EYES

Occasionally, yellow Labs have eye drainage that results in stains around the eyes. This is not necessarily a medical problem, but could be the result of blocked tear ducts. Your veterinarian may or may not be able to treat this condition. If these stains are just a cosmetic problem, you can put a drop of mineral oil in each eye and wipe the stains with a cotton ball soaked in water.

EARS

If your dog has an ear infection, it will usually give off a bad odor. You should check his ears weekly or every other week. Wipe out your dog's ears regularly with an ear cleanser. Using a cotton ball soaked in a solution, wash around the inside of the ear. If the ear is inflamed and badly infected, you should seek veterinary attention immediately.

Brushing your dog's teeth will help prevent tooth decay and keep that "doggy breath" under control.

47

To clean your dog's ears, wipe around the inside of the ear with a cotton ball soaked with ear cleanser or mineral oil.

CHAPTER SIX

Measuring Up

There really is no perfect dog: Breeders are always striving to breed dogs that come as close to the standard as possible, but when you're dealing with living creatures, the variables are numerous.

The Labrador Retriever standard was changed recently. The old as well as the new standard says the Labrador should be a medium-size dog. Balance, structure, temperament and working ability should all be considered more important than size; an otherwise good, well-balanced Labrador can't be the wrong size! This dog is now so versatile that there are needs and uses for

What constitutes a "good" Labrador is outlined in the breed's official American Kennel Club (AKC) standard. After reading a breed's standard, you should be able to visualize a well-balanced specimen of that breed.

Labradors of all sizes. Though temperament is not a physical trait, it is a hallmark of this breed. The Labrador's kindly temperament is visible in her warm eyes as well as in her body language.

The Labrador should be a medium-size dog, giving the appearance of a dog that is strong, muscular and active. The head, which includes a very specific kind and friendly expression, the coat and the tail are this breed's three outstanding characteristics. The head, coat, tail and temperament, all worn on the correct body or frame, are what give you the complete Labrador.

THE HEAD

The head is one of the breed's most distinguishing characteristics. It should not remind you of any other breed.

The Lab has a fairly broad back skull and a nice stop. The head should not have big, heavy, apple cheeks or flews that are too pendulous. The head should have a neat, clean appearance. The muzzle should be strong and never snipey looking.

The nose should be wide with well-developed nostrils, for that

WHAT IS A BREED STANDARD?

A breed standard—a detailed description of an individual breed—is meant to portray the ideal specimen of that breed. This includes ideal structure, temperament, gait and type— all aspects of the dog. Because the standard describes an ideal specimen, it isn't based on any particular dog. It is a concept against which judges compare actual dogs and breeders strive to produce dogs. At a dog show, the dog that wins is the one that comes closest, in the judge's opinion, to the standard for her breed. Breed standards are written by the breed's parent clubs, the national organizations formed to oversee the well-being of the breed. They are voted on and approved by the members of the parent clubs.

49

Regardless of how your Lab measures up against the breed standard physically, she can still make a wonderful pet and bring joy to your life.

A Labrador typically has a broad skull with medium-size ears and a generally neat, clean appearance.

keen olfactory sense. A Labrador should have what is called a "scissors bite," where the top front teeth come down right over (actually touching) the bottom front teeth. Labradors should have full dentition and should not be overshot or undershot (where there is a gap between the top and bottom jaw). Either of these conditions or a crooked jaw would make it harder for the dog to carry game.

If your dog is a family pet, it probably will not matter if her bite is not perfect. She will probably never miss a meal.

Ears

The ears should be set off the side of the skull, not too high and not too low. They should be of medium size, hanging so that the bottom tips are about 2 inches below the eyes. The ears should not be so big or so small that they draw attention to themselves. And they should never be long or folded as they are on many hounds.

Eyes

The Labrador's eyes are where we see that irresistible, sweet, kind and alert expression. The shape of the eye is like a rounded diamond. Warm brown eyes on all three colors (black, yellow or chocolate) are preferred, maybe a bit darker on a yellow Lab.

There should never be a harsh or mean look about a Labrador. When you look into a Lab's eyes, you should feel instant friendliness.

THE BODY

Neck

The desirable Labrador head should sit on a strong neck of medium length. If the neck is too short, the dog looks as if her head is sitting on her shoulders; if the neck is too long, the dog appears elegant, like a setter, which is not correct. This dog should look agile, but strong and sturdy.

As you continue down the neck, past the withers, the top line (the back) should be rather level, never swayback or sloping. The chest should be deep with well-sprung ribs like a barrel. The shoulders should be long and sloping. The correct look requires long bones that form a 90° angle as you look at the dog from the side, from the withers, to the sternum, to the elbow. The

THE AMERICAN KENNEL CLUB

Familiarly referred to as "the AKC," the American Kennel Club is a nonprofit organization devoted to the advancement of purebred dogs. The AKC maintains a registry of recognized breeds and adopts and enforces rules for dog events, including shows, obedience trials, field trials, hunting tests, lure coursing, herding, earthdog trials, agility and the Canine Good Citizen program. It is a club of clubs, established in 1884 and composed, today, of over 500 autonomous dog clubs throughout the United States. Each club is represented by a delegate; the delegates make up the legislative body of the AKC, voting on rules and electing directors. The American Kennel Club maintains the Stud Book, the record of every dog ever registered with the AKC, and publishes a variety of materials on purebred dogs, including a monthly magazine, books and numerous educational pamphlets. For more information, contact the AKC at the address listed in chapter 9.

51

front legs are well underneath the dog, allowing a prominent breastbone to show and creating the picture of a powerful chest.

Legs

All four legs should have good, thick bone, the front legs coming straight

52

Labrador Retrievers are particularly noted for the sweet, instantly friendly expression in their eyes.

down from the shoulders. The rear legs should be well bent at the knee or stifle. The hind quarters should be thick with well-muscled thighs. The hocks should not be too long and should also be well bent and well let down (not one continuous line from buttocks to the foot). The view from behind the dog should not be narrow but rather hefty with "good buns."

Tail

The tail should be set right off the back. In other words, you should see one straight line from the withers to the tip of the tail.

As a Labrador moves, the tail usually wags happily from side to side. It should never be carried curled up over the back like a hound's tail. A tail that is carried too low or between the legs will give the appearance of timidity. *Timidity* is not in the Labrador dictionary. This very important tail, which should not be too long (not below the hock), acts like a rudder when the dog is swimming. It's called an otter tail because it's thick at the base and tapers down to a tip, like the tail of an otter. The tail should be well covered with a very distinctive short, dense coat. The underside of the tail should never have any long feathery hair on it.

Coat

All three colors of the Labrador are solid colors: black, yellow or chocolate. A white spot on the chest is permissible. All the colors should have the correct double coat. The thick undercoat lies under the topcoat. The topcoat should be a bit rough to the touch and doesn't have to lie flat. In fact, if the coat is too slick, the dog probably doesn't have

Labrador Retrievers are found in one of three solid colors: black, yellow or chocolate.

a good undercoat and would not be useful as a retriever in cold waters. The undercoat acts as insulation and, working in conjunction with the coat's natural oil, helps to repel water. Therefore, the Labrador doesn't feel the cold the way a single-coated dog does.

Another aspect of this coat is the special look that it gives the Labrador. As breeder Kendall Herr says, "The Labrador has a unique stuffed-animal look, which is obtained by the double coat with a thick undercoat that fills in and rounds out any angular look." The coat makes her look like a big, 85-pound teddy bear.

THE WHOLE PICTURE

It's most important for the Labrador to be well balanced. She should not be tall and thin, and she should not be short and fat. No one feature should be so prominent as to detract from the total picture. If you look at a Labrador and notice only her huge head, the dog is probably unbalanced.

Serious breeders try very hard to take the total Labrador into consideration when thinking about breeding a litter. In choosing the right male for your female, the proper health clearances are, of course,

The overall appearance of a Labrador Retriever should be that of a well-balanced, athletic and solid-looking dog.

important, but they are just the tip of the iceberg. A breeder must know that both dogs are of sound body and mind. They must have that proper double coat, that kind expression and that otter tail, along with that wonderful, eager-to-please personality.

A good Labrador wants to please and is easy to train. She possesses a keen sense of smell and an athletic body. All these qualities make the Labrador the perfect hunting companion. Whether black, yellow or chocolate, the dog has a distinct look, singular to the Lab.

CHAPTER SEVEN

A Matter of Fact

There are many theories about the origin of the breed known today as the Labrador Retriever. One point on which all historians seem to agree is that the Labrador originally came from Newfoundland, not Labrador. They were known by several names, like the St. John's Water Dog, the Little Newfoundlander and the Black Water Dog, before officially being dubbed the Labrador Retriever.

ORIGINS OF THE LABRADOR

Some believe that the Labrador was developed by the fishermen off the coast of Newfoundland and that he was the result of an attempt to scale down the Newfoundland dog. In other words, they wanted to produce a somewhat smaller dog because the Newfies were a bit cumbersome. The dog had to be a good retriever. He also had to have good bones and strong limbs to pull heavy loads. He needed a dense coat—thick enough to withstand the cold water, but one that would not ball up with ice. He had to be eager to please, able to swim great distances and happy to live on a diet of fish and whatever else could be scrounged up. The Labrador became that dog. But how? That is the mystery.

WHERE DID DOGS COME FROM?

It can be argued that dogs were right there at man's side from the beginning of time. As soon as human beings began to document their existence, the dog was among their drawings and inscriptions. Dogs were not just friends, they served a purpose: There were dogs to hunt birds, pull sleds, herd sheep, burrow after rats—even sit in laps! What your dog was originally bred to do influences the way he behaves. The American Kennel Club recognizes over 140 breeds, and there are hundreds more distinct breeds around the world. To make sense of the breeds, they are grouped according to their size or function. The AKC has seven groups:

1. Sporting
2. Working
3. Herding
4. Hounds
5. Terriers
6. Toys
7. Nonsporting

Can you name a breed from each group? Here's some help: (1) Golden Retriever, (2) Doberman Pinscher, (3) Collie, (4) Beagle, (5) Scottish Terrier, (6) Maltese and (7) Dalmatian. All modern domestic dogs (*Canis familiaris*) are related, however different they look, and are all descended from *Canis lupus*, the gray wolf.

Scholarly Ideas

In *The Labrador Dog* by Franklin B. Lord (published privately, Labrador Retriever Club, 1945), Lord thought that "The dogs were used by the fishermen . . . to haul in the winter's wood and to retrieve fish that had become unhooked. It seems that the fish, which were taken at great depth often became unhooked near the surface and the dogs were sent overboard to retrieve them."

No one seems to know exactly when the first of these dogs arrived in England. Lord says that Lord George Scott and Leslie Sprake, authors of *The Labrador Retriever* (London, 1933), agree that ". . . it was the last decade of the 18th century or the first decade of the 19th.

Lord also tells us that there is further evidence to support these facts because the "Third Earl of Malmesbury (1807–1889) who inherited the kennel is quoted as saying 'we always called mine Labrador dogs and I have kept the breed as pure as I could from the first I had from Poole.'"

Most historians of the breed agree that the run between

The Labrador breed is thought by some to have been developed by fishermen who needed helpers that were strong, good at retrieving and that had thick, water- and cold-resistant coats.

Newfoundland and Poole Harbour, in Dorset, was a common one. The fishermen went back and forth to sell their salted codfish. The dogs often made the trip as well. Sometime around 1818, some of these dogs were seen and purchased. The English waterfowlers were quick to appreciate these talented dogs. The Second Earl of Malmesbury was said to have purchased several from some of the boats' captains. The Third Earl of Malmesbury continued to import and breed the dogs.

Although the earl said that he kept his as pure as possible, it's likely that at some point the dogs were bred with the retrievers that were being used before the fishermen arrived (to improve the local dogs). Some believe that Colonel Hawker was the first to write about the dogs and that he was actually the one to dub them Labradors; others disagree.

The Third Earl of Malmesbury gave some of his dogs to the Sixth Earl of Buccleigh, and it was he who actually started keeping good

Labrador Retrievers gained popularity as they began winning at field trials and dog shows.

breeding records. Some of our American Labs can be traced to these dogs.

In 1904, The Kennel Club (England) listed Labradors as a separate breed. Before that time, "Retriever" covered the broad category of all retrievers. Labs were gaining popularity by leaps and bounds, winning at field trials and in the ring at dog shows. In 1932 and 1933, the famous Dual Champion (Ch.) Bramshaw Bob was Best-in-Show at Crufts. Dual Ch. Bramshaw Bob was owned by the Banchory Kennel, one of the breed's most famous kennels. This kennel belonged to the late Lorna Countess Howe, remembered for doing so much to promote this breed.

About Yellow and Brown Labs

Thanks to some who liked the yellow color and made great efforts to strengthen it, we now know and enjoy yellow Labs. The late Mrs. Arthur Wormald (Veronica), of the Knaith Kennels, was one. She started the Yellow Labrador Retriever Club. Some years later, chocolates became more readily accepted as "true" Labradors.

THE LABRADOR RETRIEVER IN THE UNITED STATES

Labradors were being imported to the United States and were popular before World War I. Though the AKC grouped them together with the other retrievers, those who were active in sport shooting considered the Labrador Retrievers the best. Many serious breeders from Long Island not only imported the dogs, but they also called upon expert kennel men and gamekeepers from Europe.

By the latter part of the 1920s, the AKC recognized the Labrador Retriever as a separate breed. The Labrador Club of America was founded on Long Island late in 1930, and Mrs. Marshall Field became the first president from 1931 to 1935.

In the 1920s and 1930s, when most Labradors were dual-purpose dogs and being run in trials and were competing at bench events, many famous Long Island families were involved in these competitions. Some of the famous included the Phipps, the Marshall Fields, J. P. Morgan, Wilton Lloyd Smith and the Whitneys.

FAMOUS OWNERS OF LABRADOR RETRIEVERS

Chuck Barris	Barbara Mandrell
President Clinton	Kevin McReynolds
Gary Cooper	Queen Elizabeth
Henry Kissinger	Robert Redford
Joan Lundon	Mortimer Zuckerman

THE LAB TODAY

Today, at our Labrador Specialty Shows, it's not unusual to have an entry of 700 or more dogs. The Labrador Retriever Club of the Potomac in Leesburg, Virginia, The Miami Valley Labrador Retriever Club in Middletown, Ohio, and The Mid-Jersey Labrador Retriever Club, Heightstown, New Jersey, are probably the three biggest Lab shows in the country.

Today's Labrador show community is trying to bring about dual-, triple- and multipurpose Labradors. Club members and breeders are encouraged to strive to breed Labradors that look like and hunt like Labradors; that can do tracking tests, obedience trials and search and rescue work; that can be working

The Lab's hard-working nature, intelligence and keen sense of smell makes him perfect for work with law-enforcement officers.

companions for the handicapped and eyes for the blind; and those that can be partners for police detectives involved with narcotics, arson and explosives. A well-bred Labrador can do it all!

Hard Workers

Today, the U.S. Bureau of Alcohol, Tobacco and Firearms uses Labradors almost exclusively as explosive- and arson-sniffing dogs. They find the Lab's nose to be unrivaled by that of any other breed. And again, a Lab's willingness to please makes the dog a pleasure to work with.

Most police forces employ Labs as their drug and arson detector dogs. Most of the dogs live with the officers to whom they are assigned. Labs easily switch gears from family dogs to dependable partners in fighting crime. Their keen noses, determination and desire to please their masters have earned them great respect.

If hunting is your passion, again look no further: You have found the dog you need. Many hunters agree that because their noses are so keen and because they are so versatile, Labs make the best hunting companions. Their willingness to enter and reenter the water, no matter how cold, puts them at the head of the line in front of all other retrievers.

If you like competition and enjoy dog shows, Labs are great. They require very little grooming and should be shown in their natural state, unlike many other breeds that require hours of grooming and coat care daily or before going into the show ring. In the showring they are usually very jovial hams!

If you like obedience competition, you won't be alone if the Labrador is your choice. No matter where you live, you probably won't have to go far to find an obedience class to learn the basics. Your Labrador should have basic obedience training. You and your Labrador will both be happier for the experience.

Labradors are now the number-one breed used as guide dogs in the United States as well as in other countries. Because they are easy to groom, are so willing to please and are not easy to intimidate, Labs are perfect for this job.

Today, we are seeing more and more Labradors winning in the ring,

competing in the obedience ring and racking up titles at the AKC Hunting Retriever Tests (different from field trials—they test the dog's true hunting ability).

Labs are the number-one breed used as guide dogs in the United States.

On Good Behavior

by Ian Dunbar, Ph.D., MRCVS

Training is the jewel in the crown—the most important aspect of doggy husbandry. There is no more important variable influencing dog behavior and temperament than the dog's education: A well-trained, well-behaved and good-natured puppydog is always a joy to live with, but an untrained and uncivilized dog can be a perpetual nightmare. Moreover, deny the dog an education and she will not have the opportunity to fulfill her own canine potential; neither will she have the ability to communicate effectively with her human companions.

Luckily, modern psychological training methods are easy, efficient, effective and, above all, considerably dog-friendly and user-friendly. Doggy education is as simple as it is

enjoyable. But before you can have a good time play-training with your new dog, you have to learn what to do and how to do it. There is no bigger variable influencing the success of dog training than the owner's experience and expertise. Before you embark on the dog's education, you must first educate yourself.

BASIC TRAINING FOR OWNERS

Ideally, basic owner training should begin well before you select your dog. Find out all you can about your chosen breed first, then master rudimentary training and handling skills. If you already have your puppydog, owner training is a dire emergency—the clock is ticking! Especially for puppies, the first few weeks at home are the most important and influential days in the dog's life. Indeed, the cause of most adolescent and adult problems may be traced back to the initial days the pup explores her new home. This is the time to establish the *status quo*— to teach the puppydog how you would like her to behave and so prevent otherwise quite predictable problems.

In addition to consulting breeders and breed books such as this one (which understandably have a

Puppies can and should begin training sessions—in very short amounts— from a very young age.

positive breed bias), seek out as many pet owners with your breed as you can find. Good points are obvious. What you want to find out are the breed-specific problems, so you can nip them in the bud. In particular, you should talk to owners with adolescent dogs and make a list of all anticipated problems. Most important, test drive at least half a dozen adolescent and adult dogs of your breed yourself. An 8-week-old puppy is deceptively easy to handle, but she will acquire adult size, speed and strength in just four months, so you should learn now what to prepare for.

Puppy and pet dog training classes offer a convenient venue to locate pet owners and observe dogs in action. For a list of suitable trainers in your area, contact the Association of Pet Dog Trainers at 800-PET-DOGS.

PRINCIPLES OF TRAINING

Most people think training comprises teaching the dog to do things such as sit, speak and roll over, but even a 4-week-old pup knows how to do these things already. Instead,

the first step in training involves teaching the dog human words for each dog behavior and activity and for each aspect of the dog's environment. That way you, the owner, can more easily participate in the dog's domestic education by directing her to perform specific actions appropriately, that is, at the right time, in the right place and so on. Training opens communication channels, enabling an educated dog to at least understand her owner's requests.

In addition to teaching a dog what we want her to do, it is also necessary to teach her why she should do what we ask. Indeed, 95 percent of training revolves around motivating the dog to want to do what we want. Dogs often understand what their owners want; they just don't see the point of doing it—especially when the owner's repetitively boring and seemingly senseless instructions are totally at odds with much more pressing and exciting doggy distractions. It is not so much the dog that is being stubborn or dominant; rather, it is the owner who has failed to acknowledge the dog's needs and feelings and to approach training from the dog's point of view.

The basic training commands can be learned and effectively put to use by all members of the family.

The Meaning of Instructions

The secret to successful training is learning how to use training lures to predict or prompt specific behaviors—to coax the dog to do what you want when you want. Any highly valued object (such as a treat or toy) may be used as a lure, which the dog will follow with her eyes and nose. Moving the lure in specific ways entices the dog to

move her nose, head and entire body in specific ways. In fact, by learning the art of manipulating various lures, it is possible to teach the dog to assume virtually any body position and perform any action. Once you have control over the expression of the dog's behaviors and can elicit any body position or behavior at will, you can easily teach the dog to perform on request.

Tell your dog what you want her to do, use a lure to entice her to

A well-trained Labrador can be put to good use retrieving during a hunting trip.

respond correctly, then profusely praise and maybe reward her once she performs the desired action. For example, verbally request "Fido, sit!" while you move a squeaky toy upwards and backwards over the dog's muzzle (lure-movement and hand signal), smile knowingly as she looks up (to follow the lure) and sits down (as a result of canine anatomical engineering), then praise her to distraction ("Gooood Fido!"). Squeak the toy, offer a training treat and give your dog and yourself a pat on the back.

Being able to elicit desired responses over and over enables the owner to reward the dog over and over. Consequently, the dog begins to think training is fun. For example, the more the dog is rewarded for sitting, the more she enjoys sitting. Eventually the dog comes to realize that, whereas most sitting is appreciated, sitting immediately upon request usually prompts especially enthusiastic praise and a slew of high-level rewards. The dog begins to sit on cue much of the time, showing that she is starting to grasp the meaning of the owner's verbal request and hand signal.

Why Comply?

Most dogs enjoy initial lure-reward training and are only too happy to comply with their owners' wishes.

Unfortunately, repetitive drilling without appreciative feedback tends to diminish the dog's enthusiasm until she eventually fails to see the point of complying anymore. Moreover, as the dog approaches adolescence she becomes more easily distracted as she develops other interests. Lengthy sessions with repetitive exercises tend to bore and demotivate both parties. If it's not fun, the owner doesn't do it and neither does the dog. Integrate training into your dog's life: The greater number of training sessions each day and the shorter they are, the more willingly compliant your dog will become.

Punishment

Without a doubt, lure-reward training is by far the best way to teach: Entice your dog to do what you want and then reward her for doing so. Unfortunately, a human shortcoming is to take the good for granted and to moan and groan at the bad. Specifically, the dog's many good behaviors are ignored while the owner focuses on punishing the dog for making mistakes. In extreme cases, instruction is limited to punishing mistakes made by a trainee dog, child, employee or husband, even though it has been proven punishment training is notoriously inefficient and ineffective and is decidedly unfriendly and combative. It teaches the dog that training is a drag, almost as quickly as it teaches the dog to dislike her trainer. Why treat our best friends like our worst enemies?

Punishment training is also much more laborious and time-consuming. Whereas it takes only a finite amount of time to teach a dog what to chew, for example, it takes much, much longer to punish the dog for each and every mistake. Remember, there is only one right way! So why not teach that right way from the outset?!

To make matters worse, punishment training causes severe lapses in the dog's reliability. Since it is obviously impossible to punish the dog each and every time she misbehaves, the dog quickly learns to distinguish between those times when she must comply (so as to avoid impending punishment) and those times when she need not comply, because punishment is impossible. Such times include when the dog is off leash and 6 feet away, when the owner is otherwise engaged (talking to a

Training your dog is as much about learning what your dog's body language is telling you as it is about your dog learning what your words mean.

friend, watching television, taking a shower, tending to the baby or chatting on the telephone) or when the dog is left at home alone.

Instances of misbehavior will be numerous when the owner is away, because even when the dog complied in the owner's looming presence, she did so unwillingly. The dog was forced to act against her will, rather than molding her will to want to please. Hence, when the owner is absent, not only does the dog know she need not comply, she simply does not want to. Again, the trainee is not a stubborn vindictive beast, but rather the trainer has failed to teach. Punishment training invariably creates unpredictable Jekyll and Hyde behavior.

TRAINER'S TOOLS

Many training books extol the virtues of a vast array of training paraphernalia. In reality, most effective training tools are not found in stores; they come from within ourselves. In addition to a willing dog, all you really need is a functional human brain, gentle hands, a loving heart and a good attitude.

In terms of equipment, all dogs do require a quality buckle collar to sport dog tags and to attach the leash (for safety and to comply with local leash laws). Hollow chew toys (like Kongs or sterilized longbones) and a dog bed or collapsible crate are musts for housetraining. Three additional tools are required:

1. specific lures (training treats and toys) to predict and prompt specific desired behaviors,

2. rewards (praise, affection, training treats and toys) to reinforce for the dog what a lot of fun it all is and

3. knowledge—how to convert the dog's favorite activities and games (potential distractions to training) into "life-rewards," which may be employed to facilitate training.

The most powerful of these is knowledge. Education is the key!

HOUSETRAINING

If dogs were left to their own devices, certainly they would chew, dig and bark for entertainment and then no doubt highlight a few areas of their living space with sprinkles of urine, in much the same way we decorate by hanging pictures.

Consequently, when we ask a dog to live with us, we must teach her *where* she may dig, *where* she may perform her toilet duties, *what* she may chew and *when* she may bark. After all, when left at home alone for many hours, we cannot expect the dog to amuse herself by completing crosswords or watching the soaps on TV!

Also, it would be decidedly unfair to keep the house rules a secret from the dog and then get angry and punish the poor critter for inevitably transgressing rules she did not even know existed. Remember: Without adequate education and guidance, the dog will be forced to establish her own rules—doggy rules—and most probably will be at odds with the owner's view of domestic living.

Since most problems develop during the first few days the dog is at home, prospective dog owners must be certain they are quite clear about the principles of housetraining *before* they get a dog. Early misbehaviors quickly become established as the *status quo*—becoming firmly entrenched as hard-to-break bad habits, which set the precedent for years to come. Make sure to teach your dog good habits right from the

Your Lab will quickly learn that the appearance of a leash means a long-awaited trip outside.

Potty Training

To teach the dog where to relieve herself:

1. never let her make a single mistake,

2. let her know where you want her to go and

3. handsomely reward her for doing so: "GOOOOOOOD DOG!!!" liver treat, liver treat, liver treat!

Preventing Mistakes

A single mistake is a training disaster, since it heralds many more in future weeks. And each time the dog soils the house, this further reinforces the dog's unfortunate preference for an indoor, carpeted toilet. Do not let an unhousetrained dog have full run of the house.

start. Good habits are just as hard to break as bad ones!

Ideally, when a new dog comes home, try to arrange for someone to be present as much as possible during the first few days (for adult dogs) or weeks for puppies. With only a little forethought, it is surprisingly easy to find a puppy sitter, such as a retired person, who would be willing to eat from your refrigerator and watch your television while keeping an eye on the newcomer to encourage the dog to play with chew toys and to ensure she goes outside on a regular basis.

When you are away from home, or cannot pay full attention, confine the dog to an area where elimination is appropriate, such as an outdoor run or, better still, a small, comfortable indoor kennel with access to an outdoor run. When confined in this manner, most dogs will naturally housetrain themselves.

If that's not possible, confine the dog to an area, such as a utility room, kitchen, basement or garage, where elimination may not be desired in the long run but as an interim measure it is certainly preferable to doing it all around the house. Use newspaper to cover the floor of the dog's day room. The newspaper may be used to soak up the urine and to wrap up and dispose of the feces. Once your dog develops a preferred spot for eliminating, it is only necessary to cover that part of the floor with newspaper. The smaller papered area may then be moved (only a little each day) towards the door to the outside. Thus the dog will develop the tendency to go to the door when she needs to relieve herself.

Never confine an unhousetrained dog to a crate for long periods. Doing so would force the dog to soil the crate and ruin its usefulness as an aid for housetraining (see the following discussion).

Teaching Where

In order to teach your dog where you would like her to do her business, you have to be there to direct the proceedings—an obvious, yet often neglected, fact of life. In order to be there to teach the dog where

to go, you need to know *when* she needs to go. Indeed, the success of housetraining depends on the owner's ability to predict these times. Certainly, a regular feeding schedule will facilitate prediction somewhat, but there is nothing like "loading the deck" and influencing the timing of the outcome yourself!

Whenever you are at home, make sure the dog is under constant supervision and/or confined to a small area. If already well trained, simply instruct the dog to lie down in her bed or basket. Alternatively, confine the dog to a crate (doggy den) or tie-down (a short, 18-inch lead that can be clipped to an eye hook in the baseboard near her bed). Short-term close confinement strongly inhibits urination and defecation, since the dog does not want to soil her sleeping area. Thus, when you release the puppydog each hour, she will definitely need to urinate immediately and defecate every third or fourth hour. Keep the dog confined to her doggy den and take her to her intended toilet area each hour, every hour, on the hour. When taking your dog outside, instruct her to sit quietly before opening the door—she will soon learn to sit by the door when she needs to go out!

Teaching Why

Being able to predict when the dog needs to go enables the owner to be on the spot to praise and reward the dog. Each hour, hurry the dog to the intended toilet area in the yard, issue the appropriate instruction ("Go pee!" or "Go poop!"), then give the dog three to four minutes to produce. Praise and offer a couple of training treats when successful. The treats are important because many people fail to praise their dogs with feeling . . . and housetraining is hardly the time for understatement. So either loosen up and enthusiastically praise that dog: "Wuzzzer-wuzzer-wuzzer, hoooser good wuffer den? Hoooo went pee for Daddy?" Or say "Good dog!" as best you can and offer the treats for effect.

Following elimination is an ideal time for a spot of play-training in the yard or house. Also, an empty dog may be allowed greater freedom around the house for the next half hour or so, just as long as you keep an eye out to make sure she does not get into other kinds of mischief. If you are preoccupied and cannot pay full attention, confine the dog to her doggy den once more to enjoy a peaceful snooze or to play with her many chew toys.

If your dog does not eliminate within the allotted time outside—no biggie! Back to her doggy den, and then try again after another hour.

Beware of falling into the trap of walking the dog to get her to eliminate. The good ol' dog walk is such an enormous highlight in the dog's life that it represents the single biggest potential reward in domestic dogdom. However, when in a hurry, or during inclement weather, many owners abruptly terminate the walk the moment the dog has done her business. This, in effect, severely punishes the dog for doing the right thing, in the right place at the right time. Consequently, many dogs become strongly inhibited from eliminating outdoors because they know it will signal an abrupt end to an otherwise thoroughly enjoyable walk.

Instead, instruct the dog to relieve herself in the yard prior to going for a walk. You will find with a "No feces—no walk" policy, your dog will become one of the fastest defecators in the business.

If you do not have a backyard, instruct the dog to eliminate right outside your front door prior to the walk. Not only will this facilitate clean up and disposal of the feces in your own trash can but, also, the walk may again be used as a colossal reward.

CHEWING AND BARKING

Short-term close confinement also teaches the dog that occasional quiet moments are a reality of domestic living. Your puppydog is extremely impressionable during her first few weeks at home. Regular confinement at this time soon exerts a calming influence over the dog's personality. Remember, once the dog is house-trained and calmer, there will be a whole lifetime ahead for the dog to enjoy full run of the house and garden. On the other hand, by letting the newcomer have unrestricted access to the entire household and allowing her to run willy-nilly, she will most certainly develop a bunch of behavior problems in short order, no doubt necessitating confinement later in life.

When confining the dog, make sure she always has an impressive array of suitable chew toys. Kongs and sterilized longbones (both readily available from pet stores) make the best chew toys, because they are hollow and may be stuffed with treats to heighten the dog's interest.

Remember, treats do not have to be junk food and they certainly should not represent extra calories. Rather, treats should be part of each dog's regular daily diet: Some food may be served in the dog's bowl for breakfast and dinner, some food may be used as training treats and some food may be used for stuffing chew toys. I regularly stuff my dogs' many Kongs with different shaped biscuits and kibble. The kibble seems to fall out fairly easily, as do the oval-shaped biscuits, thus rewarding the dog instantaneously for checking out the chew toys. The bone-shaped biscuits fall out after a while, rewarding the dog for worrying at the chew toy. But the triangular bis-cuits never come out. They remain inside the Kong as lures, maintain-ing the dog's fascination with her chew toy. To further focus the dog's interest, I always make sure to flavor the triangular biscuits by rubbing them with a little cheese or freeze-dried liver.

73

If stuffed chew toys are reserved especially for times the dog is confined, the puppydog will soon learn to enjoy quiet moments in her doggy den, and she will quickly develop a chew-toy habit—a good habit! This is a simple autoshaping process; all the owner has to do is set up the situation, and the dog all but trains herself—easy and effective. Even when the dog is given run of the house, her first inclination will be to indulge her rewarding chew-toy habit rather than destroy less attractive household articles, such as curtains, carpets, chairs and compact disks. Similarly, a chew-toy chewer will be less inclined to scratch and chew herself excessively. Also, if the dog busies herself as a recreational chewer, she will be less inclined to develop into a recreational barker or digger when left at home alone.

Stuff a number of chew toys whenever the dog is left confined and remove the extra-special-tasting treats when you return. Your dog will now amuse herself with her chew toys before falling asleep and then resume playing with her chew toys when she expects you to return. Since most owner-absent misbehavior happens right after you leave and right before your expected return, your puppydog will now be conveniently preoccupied with her chew toys at these times.

COME AND SIT

Most puppies will happily approach virtually anyone, whether called or not, that is, until they collide with adolescence and develop other more important doggy interests, such as sniffing a multiplicity of exquisite odors on the grass. Your mission, Mr./Ms. Owner, is to teach and reward the pup for coming reliably, willingly and happily when called—and you have just three months to get it done. Unless adequately reinforced, your puppy's tendency to approach people will self-destruct by adolescence.

Call your dog ("Fido, come!"), open your arms (and maybe squat down) as a welcoming signal, waggle a treat or toy as a lure and reward the puppydog when she comes running. Do not wait to praise the dog until she reaches you—she may come 95 percent of the way and then run off after some distraction. Instead, praise the dog's first step towards you and continue praising enthusiastically or every step she takes in your direction.

When the rapidly approaching puppydog is three lengths away from impact, instruct her to sit ("Fido, sit!") and hold the lure in front of you in an outstretched hand to prevent her from hitting you mid-chest and knocking you flat on your back! As Fido decelerates to nose the lure, move the treat upwards and backwards just over her muzzle with an upwards motion of your extended arm (palm-upwards). As the dog looks up to follow the lure, she will sit down (if she jumps up, you are holding the lure too high). Praise the dog for sitting. Move backwards and call her again. Repeat this many times over, always praising when Fido comes and sits; on occasion, reward her.

For the first couple of trials, use a training treat both as a lure to entice the dog to come and sit and as a reward for doing so. Thereafter, try to use different items as lures and rewards. After just a few repetitions, dispense with the lures and rewards; the dog will begin to respond willingly to your verbal requests and hand signals just for the prospect of praise from your heart and affection from your hands.

Instruct every family member, friend and visitor how to get the dog to come and sit. Unless you teach your dog how to meet people, that is, to sit for greetings, no doubt the dog will resort to jumping up. Then you and the visitors will get annoyed, and the dog will be punished. This is not fair.

To teach come, call your dog, open your arms as a welcoming signal, wave a toy or a treat and praise for every step in your direction.

Even though your dog quickly masters obedient recalls in the house, her reliability may falter when playing in the backyard or local park. Ironically, it is the owner who has unintentionally trained the dog not to respond in these instances. By allowing the dog to play and run around and otherwise have a good time, but then to call the dog to put her on leash to take her home, the dog quickly learns playing is fun but training is a drag. Thus, playing in the park becomes a severe distraction, which works against training. Bad news!

Instead, whether playing with the dog off leash or on leash, request her to come at frequent intervals—say, every minute or so. On most occasions, praise and pet the dog for a few seconds while she is sitting, then tell her to go play again. For especially fast recalls, offer a couple of training treats and take the time to praise and pet the dog enthusiastically before releasing her. The dog will learn that coming when called is not necessarily the end of the play session, and neither is it the end of the world; rather, it signals an enjoyable, quality time-out with the owner before resuming play once more. In fact, playing in the park

now becomes a very effective life-reward, which works to facilitate training by reinforcing each obedient and timely recall. Good news!

SIT, DOWN, STAND AND ROLL OVER

Teaching the dog a variety of body positions is easy for owner and dog, impressive for spectators and extremely useful for all. Using lure-reward techniques, it is possible to train several positions at once to verbal commands or hand signals (which impress the socks off of onlookers).

Sit and down—the two control commands—prevent or resolve nearly a hundred behavior problems. For example, if the dog happily and obediently sits or lies down when requested, she cannot jump on visitors, dash out the front door, run around and chase her tail, pester other dogs, harass cats or annoy family, friends or strangers. Additionally, "Sit" or "Down" are the best emergency commands for off-leash control.

It is easier to teach and maintain a reliable sit than maintain a reliable recall. Sit is the purest and simplest of commands—either the dog is sitting or she is not. If there is any change of circumstances or potential danger in the park, for example, simply instruct the dog to sit. If she sits, you have a number of options: Allow the dog to resume playing when she is safe, walk up and put the dog on leash or call the dog. The dog will be much more likely to come when called if she has already acknowledged her compliance by sitting. If the dog does not sit in the park—train her to!

Stand and roll over-stay are the two positions for examining the dog. Your veterinarian will love you to distraction if you take a little time to teach the dog to stand still and roll over and play possum.

As with teaching come and sit, the training techniques to teach the dog to assume all other body positions on cue are user-friendly and dog-friendly. Simply give the appropriate request, lure the dog into the desired body position using a training treat or toy and then praise (and maybe reward) the dog as soon as she complies. Try not to touch the dog to get her to respond. If you teach the dog by guiding her into position, the dog will quickly learn that rump-pressure means sit, for example, but as yet you still have no control over

your dog if she is just 6 feet away. It will still be necessary to teach the dog to sit on request. So do not make training a time-consuming two-step process; instead, teach the dog to sit to a verbal request or hand signal from the outset. Once the dog sits willingly when requested, by all means use your hands to pet the dog when she does so.

To teach down when the dog is already sitting, say "Fido, down!," hold the lure in one hand (palm down) and lower that hand to the floor between the dog's forepaws. As the dog lowers her head to follow the lure, slowly move the lure away from the dog just a fraction (in front of her paws). The dog will lie down as she stretches her nose forward to follow the lure. Praise the dog when she does so. If the dog stands up, you pulled the lure away too far and too quickly.

When teaching the dog to lie down from the standing position, say "Down" and lower the lure to the floor as before. Once the dog has lowered her forequarters and assumed a play bow, gently and slowly move the lure towards the dog between her forelegs. Praise the dog as soon as her rear end plops down.

77

Using a food lure to teach sit, down and stand.
1) "Phoenix, sit."
2) Hand palm upwards, move lure up and back over dog's muzzle.
3) "Good sit, Phoenix!"

4) "Phoenix, down." 5) Hand palm down- wards, move lure down to lie between dog's forepaws.
6) "Phoenix, off. Good down, Phoenix!"

7) "Phoenix, sit!"
8) Palm upwards, move lure up and back, keeping it close to dog's muzzle.
9) "Good sit, Phoenix!"

10) *"Phoenix, stand!"*

11) *Move lure away from dog at nose height, then lower it a tad.*

12) *"Phoenix, off! Good stand, Phoenix!"*

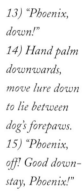

79

13) *"Phoenix, down!"*

14) *Hand palm downwards, move lure down to lie between dog's forepaws.*

15) *"Phoenix, off! Good down-stay, Phoenix!"*

16) *"Phoenix, stand!"*

17) *Move lure away from dog's muzzle up to nose height.*

18) *"Phoenix, off! Good stand-stay, Phoenix.*

You will notice the more energetically you move your arm—upwards (palm up) to get the dog to sit, and downwards (palm down) to get the dog to lie down—the more energetically the dog responds to your requests. Now try training the dog in silence and you will notice she has also learned to respond to hand signals. Yeah! Not too shabby for the first session.

To teach stand from the sitting position, say "Fido, stand," slowly move the lure half a dog-length away from the dog's nose, keeping it at nose level, and praise the dog as she stands to follow the lure. As soon as the dog stands, lower the lure to just beneath the dog's chin to entice her to look down; otherwise she will stand and then sit immediately. To prompt the dog to stand from the down position, move the lure half a dog-length upwards and away from the dog, holding the lure at standing nose height from the floor.

Teaching roll over is best started from the down position, with the dog lying on one side, or at least with both hind legs stretched out on the same side. Say "Fido, bang!" and move the lure backwards and along-side the dog's muzzle to her elbow (on the side of her outstretched hind legs). Once the dog looks to the side and backwards, very slowly move the lure upwards to the dog's shoulder and backbone. Tickling the dog in the goolies (groin area) often invokes a reflex-raising of the hind leg as an appeasement gesture, which facilitates the tendency to roll over. If you move the lure too quickly and the dog jumps into the standing position, have patience and start again. As soon as the dog rolls onto her back, keep the lure stationary and mesmerize the dog with a relaxing tummy rub.

To teach roll over-stay when the dog is standing or moving, say "Fido, bang!" and give the appropriate hand signal (with index finger pointed and thumb cocked in true Sam Spade fashion), then in one fluid movement lure her to first lie down and then roll over-stay as above.

Teaching the dog to stay in each of the above four positions becomes a piece of cake after first teaching the dog not to worry at the toy or treat training lure. This is best accomplished by hand feeding dinner kibble. Hold a piece of kibble

firmly in your hand and softly instruct "Off!" Ignore any licking and slobbering for however long the dog worries at the treat, but say "Take it!" and offer the kibble *the instant* the dog breaks contact with her muzzle. Repeat this a few times, and then up the ante and insist the dog remove her muzzle for one whole second before offering the kibble. Then progressively refine your criteria and have the dog not touch your hand (or treat) for longer and longer periods on each trial, such as for two seconds, four seconds, then six, ten, fifteen, twenty, thirty seconds and so on.

The dog soon learns: (1) worrying at the treat never gets results,

whereas (2) noncontact is often rewarded after a variable time lapse.

Teaching "Off!" has many useful applications in its own right. Additionally, instructing the dog not to touch a training lure often produces spontaneous and magical stays. Request the dog to stand-stay, for example, and not to touch the lure. At first set your sights on a short two-second stay before rewarding the dog. (Remember, every long journey begins with a single step.) However, on subsequent trials, gradually and progressively increase the length of stay required to receive a reward. In no time at all your dog will stand calmly for a minute or so.

Teaching your dog basic commands like stay will employ a few simple hand signals.

RELEVANCY TRAINING

Once you have taught the dog what you expect her to do when requested to come, sit, lie down, stand, roll over and stay, the time is right to teach the dog why she should comply with your wishes. The secret is to have many (many) extremely short training interludes (two to five seconds each) at numerous times during the course of the dog's day.

In no time at all the dog will be only too pleased to follow your instructions because she has learned that a compliant response heralds all sorts of goodies. Basically all you are trying to teach the dog is how to say please: "Please throw the tennis ball. Please may I snuggle on the couch."

In fact, the dog may be unable to distinguish between training and good times, and, indeed, there should be no distinction. The warped concept that training involves forcing the dog to comply and/or dominating her will is totally at odds with the picture of a truly well-trained dog. In reality, enjoying a game of training with a dog is no different from enjoying a game of backgammon or tennis with a friend; and walking with a dog should be no different from strolling with a spouse or with buddies on the golf course.

WALK BY YOUR SIDE

Many people attempt to teach a dog to heel by putting her on a leash and physically correcting the dog when she makes mistakes. There are a number of things seriously wrong with this approach, the first being that most people do not want precision heeling; rather, they simply want the dog to follow or walk by their side. Second, when physically restrained during "training," even though the dog may grudgingly mope by your side when "handcuffed" on leash, let's see what happens when she is off leash. History! The dog is in the next county because she never enjoyed walking with you on leash, and you have no control over her off leash. So let's just teach the dog off leash from the outset to want to walk with us. Third, if the dog has not been trained to heel, it is a trifle hasty to think about punishing the poor dog for making mistakes and breaking heeling rules she didn't even know existed. This is simply not fair!

Surely, if the dog had been adequately taught how to heel, she would seldom make mistakes and hence there would be no need to correct the dog. Remember, each mistake and each correction (punishment) advertise the trainer's inadequacy, not the dog's. The dog is not stubborn, she is not stupid and she is not bad. Even if she were, she would still require training, so let's train her properly.

Let's teach the dog to enjoy following us and to want to walk by our side off leash. Then it will be easier to teach high-precision off-leash heeling patterns if desired. Before going on outdoor walks, it is necessary to teach the dog not to pull. Then it becomes easy to teach on-leash walking and heeling because the dog already wants to walk with you, she is familiar with the desired walking and heeling positions and she knows not to pull.

FOLLOWING

Start by training your dog to follow you. Many puppies will follow if you simply walk away from them and maybe click your fingers or chuckle. Adult dogs may require additional enticement to stimulate them to follow, such as a training lure or, at the very least, a lively trainer. To teach the dog to follow: (1) keep walking and (2) walk away from the dog. If the dog attempts to lead or lag, change pace; slow down if the dog forges too far ahead, but speed up if she lags too far behind. Say "Steady!" or "Easy!" each time before you slow down and "Quickly!" or "Hustle!" each time before you speed up, and the dog will learn to change pace on cue. If the dog lags or leads too far, or if she wanders right or left, simply walk quickly in the opposite direction and maybe even run away from the dog and hide.

Practicing is a lot of fun; you can set up a course in your home, yard or park to do this. Indoors, entice the dog to follow upstairs, into a bedroom, into the bathroom, downstairs, around the living room couch, zigzagging between dining room chairs and into the kitchen for dinner. Outdoors, get the dog to follow around park benches, trees, shrubs and along walkways and lines in the grass. (For safety outdoors, it is advisable to attach a long line on the dog, but never exert corrective tension on the line.)

Remember, following has a lot to do with attitude—your attitude!

Most probably your dog will not want to follow Mr. Grumpy Troll with the personality of wilted lettuce. Lighten up—walk with a jaunty step, whistle a happy tune, sing, skip and tell jokes to your dog, and she will be there by your side.

BY YOUR SIDE

It is smart to train the dog to walk close on one side or the other—either side will do, your choice. When walking, jogging or cycling, it is generally bad news to have the dog suddenly cut in front of you. In fact, I train my dogs to walk "By my side" and "Other side"—both very useful instructions. It is possible to position the dog fairly accurately by looking to the appropriate side and clicking your fingers or slapping your thigh on that side. A precise positioning may be attained by holding a training lure, such as a chew toy, tennis ball, or food treat. Stop and stand still several times throughout the walk, just as you would when window shopping or meeting a friend. Use the lure to make sure the dog slows down and stays close whenever you stop.

When teaching the dog to heel, we generally want her to sit in heel position when we stop. Teach heel position at the standstill, and the dog will learn that the default heel position is sitting by your side (left or right—your choice, unless you wish to compete in obedience trials, in which case the dog must heel on the left).

Several times a day, stand up and call your dog to come and sit in heel position—"Fido, heel!" For example, instruct the dog to come to heel each time there are commercials on TV or each time you turn a page of a novel, and the dog will get it in a single evening.

Practice straight-line heeling and turns separately. With the dog sitting at heel, teach her to turn in place. After each quarter-turn, half-turn or full turn in place, lure the dog to sit at heel. Now it's time for short straight-line heeling sequences, no more than a few steps at a time. Always think of heeling in terms of sit-heel-sit sequences—start and end with the dog in position and do your best to keep her there when moving. Progressively increase the number of steps in each sequence. When the dog remains close for 20 yards of straight-line heeling, it is time to add a few turns and then sign up for a happy-heeling obedience class to get some advice from the experts.

NO PULLING ON LEASH

You can start teaching your dog not to pull on leash anywhere—in front of the television or outdoors—but regardless of location, you must not take a single step with tension in the leash. For a reason known only to dogs, even just a couple of paces of pulling on leash is intrinsically motivating and diabolically rewarding. Instead, attach the leash to the dog's collar, grasp the other end firmly with both hands held close to your chest, and stand still—do not budge an inch. Have somebody watch you with a stopwatch to time your progress, or else you will never believe this will work and so you will not even try the exercise, and your shoulder and the dog's neck will be traumatized for years to come.

Stand still and wait for the dog to stop pulling and to sit and/or lie down. All dogs stop pulling and sit eventually. Most take only a couple of minutes; the all-time record is $22^1/_2$ minutes. Time how long it takes. Gently praise the dog when she stops pulling, and as soon as she

sits, enthusiastically praise the dog and take just one step forwards, then immediately stand still. This single step usually demonstrates the ballistic reinforcing nature of pulling on leash; most dogs explode to the end of the leash, so be prepared for the strain. Stand firm and wait for the dog to sit again. Repeat this half a dozen times, and you will probably notice a progressive reduction in the force of the dog's one-step explosions and a radical reduction in the time it takes for the dog to sit each time.

As the dog learns "Sit we go" and "Pull we stop," she will begin to walk forward calmly with each single step and automatically sit when you stop. Now try two steps before you stop. Wooooooo! Scary! When the dog has mastered two steps at a time, try for three. After each success, progressively increase the number of steps in the sequence: Try four steps and then six, eight, ten and twenty steps before stopping. Congratulations! You are now walking the dog on leash.

Whenever walking with the dog (off leash or on leash), make sure you stop periodically to practice a few position commands and stays before instructing the dog to "Walk on!" (Remember, you want the dog to be compliant everywhere, not just in the kitchen when her dinner is at hand.) For example, stopping every 25 yards to briefly train the dog amounts to over 200 training interludes within a single 3-mile stroll. And each training session is in a different location. You will not believe the improvement within just the first mile of the first walk.

To put it another way, integrating training into a walk offers 200 separate opportunities to use the continuance of the walk as a reward to reinforce the dog's education. Moreover, some training interludes may comprise continuing education for the dog's walking skills: Alternate short periods of the dog walking calmly by your side with periods when the dog is allowed to sniff and investigate the environment. Now sniffing odors on the grass and meeting other dogs become rewards that reinforce the dog's calm and mannerly demeanor. Good Lord! Whatever next? Many enjoyable walks together of course. Happy trails!

Further Reading

BOOKS

About Labrador Retrievers

Churchill, Janet I. *The New Labrador Retriever.* New York: Howell Book House, 1995.

About Health Care

American Kennel Club. *American Kennel Club Dog Care and Training.* New York: Howell Book House, 1991.

Carlson, Delbert, DVM, and James Giffen, MD. *Dog Owner's Home Veterinary Handbook.* New York: Howell Book House, 1992.

DeBitetto, James, DVM, and Sarah Hodgson. *You & Your Puppy.* New York: Howell Book House, 1995.

Humphries, Jim, DVM. *Dr. Jim's Animal Clinic for Dogs.* New York: Howell Book House, 1994.

Pitcairn, Richard and Susan. *Natural Health for Dogs.* Emmaus, Pa.: Rodale Press, 1982.

Schwartz, Stefanie, DVM. *First Aid for Dogs: An Owner's Guide to a Happy Healthy Pet.* New York: Howell Book House, 1998.

About Training

Ammen, Amy. *Training in No Time.* New York: Howell Book House, 1995.

Dunbar, Ian, Ph.D, MRCVS. *Dr. Dunbar's Good Little Book.* James & Kenneth Publishers, 2140 Shattuck Ave. #2406, Berkeley, Calif. 94704. (510) 658-8588. Order from publisher.

————. *How to Teach a New Dog Old Tricks.* James & Kenneth Publishers. Order from the publisher; address above.

Dunbar, Ian, Ph.D, MRCVS, and Gwen Bohnenkamp. *Booklets on Preventing Aggression; Housetraining; Chewing; Digging; Barking; Socialization; Fearfulness; and Fighting.* James & Kenneth Publishers. Order from the publisher; address above.

Evans, Job Michael. *People, Pooches and Problems.* New York: Howell Book House, 1991.

About Activities

American Rescue Dog Association. *Search and Rescue Dogs.* New York: Howell Book House, 1991.

Daniels, Julie. *Enjoying Dog Agility—From Backyard to Competition.* New York: Doral Publishing, 1990.

O'Neil, Jackie. *All About Agility.* New York: Howell Book House, 1998.

Simmons-Moake, Jane. *Agility Training. The Fun Sport for All Dogs.* New York: Howell Book House, 1991.

Volhard, Jack and Wendy. *The Canine Good Citizen.* New York: Howell Book House, 1994.

MAGAZINES

THE AKC GAZETTE, The Official Journal for the Sport of Purebred Dogs
American Kennel Club
51 Madison Ave.
New York, NY 10010.

DOG FANCY
Fancy Publications
3 Burroughs
Irvine, CA 92718.

DOG WORLD
Maclean Hunter Publishing Corp.
29 N. Wacker Dr.
Chicago, IL 60606.

RESOURCES

The American Kennel Club

The American Kennel Club, devoted to the advancement of purebred dogs, is the oldest and largest registry organization in this country. Every breed recognized by the AKC has a national (parent) club. National clubs are a great source of information on your breed. The affiliated clubs hold AKC events and use AKC rules to hold performance events, dog shows, educational programs, health clinics and training classes. The AKC staff is divided between offices in New York City and Raleigh, North Carolina. All registration functions are done in North Carolina.

For registration and performance events information, contact:

THE AMEICAN KENNEL CLUB
5580 Centerview Dr., Suite 200
Raleigh, NC 27606
Phone: (919) 233-9767; Fax: (919) 233-3767
E-mail: info@akc.org

For obedience information, contact:

THE AMERICAN KENNEL CLUB
51 Madison Ave.
New York, NY 10010
Phone: (212) 696-8276
Fax: (212) 696-8272
E-mail: www.akc.org

For information on AKC Companion Animal Recovery, contact:

Phone: (800) 252-7894
Fax: (919) 233-1290
E-mail: found@akc.org

Registry Organizations

UNITED KENNEL CLUB (UKC)
100 E. Kilgore Road
Kalamazoo, MI 49002

CANADIAN KENNEL CLUB
100-89 Skyway Ave.
Etobicoke, Ontario
Canada M9W 6R4

Activity Clubs

Write to these organizations for information on the activities they sponsor.

UNITED KENNEL CLUB
100 E. Kilgore Rd.
Kalamazoo, MI 49002
(Conformation Shows, Obedience Trials, Agility, Hunting for Various
Breeds, Terrier Trials and more.)

INTERNATIONAL SLED DOG RACING ASSOCIATION
P.O. Box 446
Nordman, ID 83838

Trainers

ASSOCIATION OF PET DOG TRAINERS
P.O. Box 385
Davis, CA 95617
800-PET-DOGS